Guide to Re-building Trust with Traumatised Children

At times children are unable or unwilling to access or engage with emotional and mental health support services. Often members of a child's support network are therefore required to provide this emotional guidance and support to them. This resource book is intended to be used as a guide by families and friends, school staff, and any other adults supporting children who have experienced trauma, to help the adults to provide the emotional guidance these children need.

Guide to Re-building Trust with Traumatised Children aims to educate the reader about trauma and the impact of an insecure attachment – how it may impact a child, how to support a child – as well as helping the reader to understand different behaviours. The guide suggests many practical ideas and activities designed to help children to build more positive relationships, to feel safe within their world, and to express and explore their emotions. There is a section on self-care for adults, and advice about when a referral to a specialist service may be required.

This guide was designed to be used by any person supporting a child who has experienced trauma or an insecure attachment, no matter what their previous understanding of these issues might be. It is specifically written to be as accessible and as user friendly as possible to help rather than hinder the user. It can be used alone or together with the storybook *The House That Wouldn't Fall Down*.

Hollie Rankin is a counsellor who has worked with and supported children, young people and their families within schools in the North East over the last ten years. Her recent books on trauma and bereavement were prompted by a noticeable gap in resources to help to guide adults when supporting children in emotionally challenging circumstances.

Guide to Re-building Trust with Traumatised Children

Emotional Wellbeing in School and at Home

HOLLIE RANKIN

Routledge
Taylor & Francis Group

LONDON AND NEW YORK

First published 2019
by Routledge
2 Park Square, Milton Park, Abingdon, Oxon OX14 4RN

and by Routledge
52 Vanderbilt Avenue, New York, NY 10017

Routledge is an imprint of the Taylor & Francis Group, an informa business

British Library Cataloguing-in-Publication Data
A catalogue record for this book is available from the British Library

Library of Congress Cataloging-in-Publication Data
Names: Rankin, Hollie, author. | Rankin, Hollie. companion volume. House that wouldn't fall down,
Title: Guide to re-building trust with traumatised children : emotional wellbeing in school and at home / Hollie Rankin.
Description: Abingdon, Oxon ; New York, NY : Routledge, 2019. | Companion to the storybook: The house that wouldn't fall down.
Identifiers: LCCN 2018057140 | ISBN 9781138360471 (pbk) | ISBN 9780429433122 (ebk)
Subjects: LCSH: Psychic trauma in children. | Trust in children. | Children—Mental health. | School mental health services.
Classification: LCC RJ506.P66 R36 2019 | DDC 618.92/8521—dc23
LC record available at https://lccn.loc.gov/2018057140

ISBN: 978-1-138-36047-1 (pbk)
ISBN: 978-0-429-43312-2 (ebk)

Typeset in Antitled
by Apex CoVantage, LLC

I would like to thank everyone who helped in the creation of this book. I would particularly like to thank Corrin and Deb who started this publishing journey off when I wasn't brave enough to, and my Dad for the countless hours of support and endless advice during the writing of my first-ever books.

I would like to dedicate this book to the many children I have had the honour of supporting, who have let me into their lives during some of their most difficult times.
The most resilient and courageous children you could ever know.

Contents

Introduction

I began working in schools as a counsellor almost ten years ago. I have had the pleasure of working with some of the most wonderful children it has been my honour to meet. Some of these children had experienced the most adverse circumstances, and still demonstrated a level of resilience that I certainly could never have mustered in a similar situation.

Each counselling session was only 45 minutes out of each child's week. Although it helped many children, this was certainly not the only factor making that crucial difference. The children I supported spent on average 32 hours per week at school, and many more waking hours at home, but less than one with me in a counselling session. There had to be other forces at play here, other explanations for how the emotional difficulties of some of these children decreased and their emotional intelligence and coping strategies increased.

There was and could be only one explanation ... the child's inner resilience mixed with the hard work, patience and dedication of their parents, carers, family members, social workers, support workers, teachers and teaching assistants. These children needed repetitive, reliable and constant intervention on a minute-by-minute basis – all day, every day – and these were the people delivering this vital resource and supporting the child's therapy.

As we all know, budgets are being cut across many much-needed services, including schools and mental health services. The impact of this is that our children are not always able to access emotional support from a counsellor, or external agencies. More and more often, this emotional support is being put onto the shoulders of parents, carers, support workers and school staff. These people are absolutely in the strongest position to help children to make changes as they are with them daily, and this is the key to helping a child's brain to adapt, develop and begin to forge new connections.

Much work can be done in schools and within the home to help children to explore and express their emotions, and I fully believe these skills need to be taught to all children by all involved, not just those in the counselling room.

This book is not intended as an alternative to therapy, but as an *addition* to it. These activities and exercises are designed to support children in exploring and managing big emotions with the people they are closest to. You, as families and professionals, already do this with the children on a daily basis. This book is intended to provide some further guidance and ideas that will hopefully help and support you as you continue in this hugely important role.

This book, of course, was written first and foremost for children, for the vulnerable young people, who continue to astound me daily in so many weird, wonderful and wacky ways. But it was also written for the people who may not have a formal qualification in psychology or counselling, but who are still expected to support these children emotionally, and understand their behaviour, however baffling it may be. It was written for the people who, despite the overwhelming number of other responsibilities and demands on them, are expected to do all of this with remarkably little support and time, and who continue to put their hearts and souls into our children.

This work is dedicated to those people without whom the children's worlds would be harsher, lonelier and friendless places. Together we can be their vast, caring family and help them to find a better way.

'The child who is not embraced by the village will burn it down to feel its warmth.'
– African proverb

Considerations

Please bear in mind that not all activities may be suitable for all children. Elements may need to be changed or adapted to suit a child's age and level of understanding, and some may not be suitable at all for certain children. Activities and information need to be explained using appropriate language, taking into consideration the child's developmental age, not just their chronological age.

One of our aims is to increase the confidence of the children we work with, particularly those who may struggle to succeed in other areas. This includes helping them to succeed at the tasks they take part in. If we can pitch activities at a level where each child is able to be successful, we can help build their confidence, and increase their chances of continuing to 'take risks' – risks with the activities and risks in engaging in the relationship with us.

It is really not important for children to worry about spelling, handwriting, or being neat and tidy when taking part in these activities. Even if you are school-based, try to suspend your beliefs about the importance of these issues just for a while – teachers, you know who you are! Feelings are rarely neat and tidy, so why should the expression of them be?

If you know that a child struggles with spelling or hates writing then you could offer to do any writing on their behalf, or select activities that don't involve any literacy. If there is some element of literacy involved, you could encourage them to try by giving them every assurance that presentation and spelling are really not important. In fact, as long as the child knows what they have written, then that is really all that matters: no one else needs to see it. And reassure them that it really does *not* matter to you – whatever you do, don't point out any mistakes.

Some of the exercises ask that the child closes their eyes. The reason for this is that closing your eyes can be relaxing (for some), as it helps to reduce sensory distractions from the world around, and allows you to focus on what you are hearing rather than seeing. It can also help children to process information as it reduces sensory input.

However, for many different reasons, a child might not wish to do this. To close your eyes in the presence of another can leave you feeling vulnerable – there needs to be an element of trust with the other person, of trust that they are safe. It may be that having their eyes closed links back to previous negative experiences, or it might leave a child feeling a sense of being out of control or helpless. There are many reasons why a child might not want to close their eyes, and we need to respect their decision.

After completing activities with children, it is important to ensure that it is possible for them to take some extra time to process their emotions, so that they are not left in a distressed state, or feeling vulnerable.

When supporting children you might need to consider an onward referral to a mental health service. It can be helpful to know your local referral system and how to access other services, particularly when children need to receive in-depth one-to-one support. Children may also need someone fighting their corner to ensure that they accepted into services in order to get the support they require.

1. Trauma and attachment

Who is this book for?

This book was written to support children who have experienced developmental trauma. Children who have experience of the care system are often most at risk of having experienced developmental trauma, which can severely impact their development in every way. This is often further compounded by many moves within the care system, and the experience of never having had an opportunity to develop a secure base from which to begin to attempt to overcome such extreme adversity. Many children who have not been in Local Authority Care may also have experienced developmental trauma for a variety of different reasons.

Where children have experienced developmental trauma, a whole community approach is required – school, home and therapy working together in the same way to support the child. There are, however, many things that the adults around these children can do in order to support them emotionally during therapy, as well as before and after the intervention. The people in the best position to be able to promote change within a child are those the child spends the most time with, as children need consistent, reliable and persistent input in order to make changes. *You* are the very people that children spend the most time with.

Attachment

I'm sure that most of you will have heard of the term 'attachment', a theory developed by John Bowlby in the 1950s. There are many books, articles, websites and videos about attachment theory, so I am just going to touch on it briefly in this book. My main aim for this book is to suggest ways of working with children, not necessarily focusing on theories, which can be looked at separately.

John Bowlby said that human beings naturally seek to establish a strong emotional bond with their primary caregiver, as well as seeking safety and support from this person. The early years of a child's life are the most crucial. The infant needs to experience a consistent, reliable, warm, safe and intimate relationship with this person. If their needs are responded to, if the caregiver is available both physically and emotionally, and if the child experiences empathy, then the child is more likely to develop in a healthy manner in terms of their social, emotional, physical and intellectual development. This parental bonding creates neural pathways in the infant's brain. This positive, secure bond helps the infant to learn to trust others and form positive relationships, as they have learned that people can be trusted, and their needs will be met. Bowlby described this positive early experience as having a 'secure base'.

There are many reasons that the relationship with the primary caregiver may not be secure: parental mental health difficulties, divorce, substance misuse, and bereavement, are just some examples. When the attachment relationship is compromised, or the child is stressed, it can impact greatly on a child's development. The child may develop what Bowlby called an 'insecure base', which can impact the normal development of the brain because the development of neural pathways can be affected. Children are often unable to self-regulate and self-soothe. They can be prone to fight, flight or freeze survival responses when their systems become overwhelmed and they are frequently unable to manage threat, real or perceived. Remember that, due to their early experiences, these children are much more likely to perceive things as threatening even if they are not.

Academic performance, self-esteem, as well trust in the world and other people, can all be impacted. Children can struggle to make and maintain relationships, can lack an ability to empathise, and can struggle with impulsivity and social responsibility. They often function at a developmental age lower than their chronological age, further compounding their difficulties – as their peers often move further away from them in terms of development.

We all have an 'attachment style' based on our early experiences. There are different styles of attachment, and these different styles can affect how children relate to the world and others around them.

Trauma

Trauma is the result of events that overwhelm us and our ability to cope. It can incite feelings of helplessness, fear and terror. Many children are able to recover from trauma, particularly where the trauma was linked to a one-time event, however, even when children have a secure base and support, there are some who will struggle to overcome trauma, and this may result in longer-term emotional difficulties.

Trauma linked to repeated events, such as domestic abuse, appears to cause the most long-term emotional damage, particularly where the child believes, at the time, there is a significant risk of injury or death to them or others, let alone if they or a loved one are actually injured.

2. Supporting children

What can we do?

One of the best things we can do for children who have experienced developmental trauma and/or who have an insecure base is to help them to build connections between the different parts of their brain. In particular, help them to learn how to regulate their 'cave' or primitive brain and to re-engage their 'thinking brain'.

The activities and exercises throughout this book help to support this outcome. I have also outlined some of these ways below.

Environment

It is important for us all to consider how a child is impacted by the environment they are in. In order for any changes at all to take place, the child needs to be in a safe environment. Children who have suffered developmental trauma become stuck in the brain stem, in the 'cave' or 'survival' brain, where they are hyper-alert to danger at all times in order to stay alive and survive. These children can often struggle to learn in a classroom environment and they require repetitive, persistent and consistent activities over time to help to calm their fear responses and to help to repair their brains.

Taking a school/home approach where trauma is the focus can be hugely beneficial for children with developmental trauma, and providing an environment that is suitable for them also benefits children who do not have any additional needs. Such environments are healthy places for us all.

You could start with a sensory audit, and try to experience the environment from the child's perspective. Ensure that the environment is organised around the child's brain age and not their chronological age, as the two can be very different. It is important to ensure that environments are not overstimulating by limiting distractions and other stimuli. It might be that there are too many brightly coloured displays in a classroom, or that a child's bedroom has too much furniture. Try to keep things simple, and use storage to avoid clutter.

There are many things that can cause alarm for these children – things that a person not coming from a trauma perspective may not deem to be scary or overwhelming. Children who have experienced trauma and an insecure attachment are often hyper-vigilant and constantly on the 'look out' (in every sense – not just looking) for danger.

Key person

If we can create an environment where the child feels calm, safe and secure, it is then that we can begin to help them to make changes. Children are unable to grow, learn and develop when they are trapped in a place of fear and trauma. In order to feel safe, children need continuity, routine and stability from calm, caring adults. Identifying a key adult for the child at home and at school is crucial to their development. These key people can have the most positive input in helping children to change the way they experience the world and actually encourage new neural pathways to develop within the brain.

For many infants the caregiver is so in tune with them that they are able to do this before the infant has even signalled a need. For example, this may happen when a parent provides a bottle knowing that the baby will be getting hungry, or senses they may be restless and picks them up to soothe them, or puts them down for a nap before the child cries to signal they are tired. Often, as infants, children with developmental trauma did not experience their needs being anticipated and responded to by a caregiver.

If key adults can anticipate and respond to the needs of the child without the child having to do anything to signal this, then the intention is that the child will eventually begin to learn that they can rely on others. The hope would then be that the child could become less focused and anxious about having their needs met, and begin to develop an ability to focus on other things.

People who see the child daily are ideal for this role, but we should also take into account that these people need to be up for the challenge, resilient and emotionally stable, as well as have the time to commit and actually want the role. Most importantly, check that the identified people like the child. The likelihood is that the child will do everything in their power to try to get the person to *not* like them, and it can be at times like these that a key adult needs to hold on to those nuggets of gold, and remember the child they like, the child they enjoy being with, the child who they are doing this for.

Often children will test the adults and the boundaries around them in order to see if those adults really will continue to be the calm, reliable humans that they are demonstrating – remember, the child is likely to have been let down in many ways and many times by the people they should be able to rely on – why would they believe that you are any different? After all, that is what they have learned that adults do. They may test your 'staying power', test to see if you actually care, and if you can manage, and still care for them, at their worst by displaying many challenging behaviours. Often it is the adults that the child is beginning to develop a relationship with who take the brunt of the difficult behaviour, and this can escalate as the child grows closer to the adult.

I once worked with a boy who would tell me to go away when I saw him around school – even if I wasn't actually near him, but then he would later come to find me and ask me to look after his pen lid or his headphones.

As the key person it is vital that you are many things, including reliable, warm, consistent, calm and caring. You need to demonstrate to the child that you care, are interested, have time for them, and that they are important to you. You also need to demonstrate that you are still engaged in a relationship with the child despite their behaviour. Doing what you say is imperative, as letting these children down can be hugely damaging; and can easily be done unintentionally, so try to remain mindful of this.

For two years, I had daily contact with a young girl who was living in a foster-care placement. I spent time with her five days a week, every single week, just to catch up and check in. I was consistent and reliable, until one day when my son was poorly and I needed to take a day off work. When I returned she was furious with me, she told me how I 'always' let her down and 'never' did what I said I would. She experienced this as me abandoning her and letting her down 'just like everyone else had'. Even a year later she would still remind me of the one day I wasn't there. To me it was one day, to her it was everything.

Unavoidable things do happen from time to time, things out of your control, and as a result there is likely to be reparation work to do with the child, and hopefully you can both move on together from it. It can be an opportunity to model that you made a mistake, by owning it, being honest, apologising, and working on repairing the relationship. Opportunities like this can be challenging for both parties, but it can help the child to see that you are human, that humans do make mistakes from time to time, and that your relationship can be repaired and survive.

There are so many things that can be avoided, however. There are so many ways we can ensure that we *don't* let the child down and become inconsistent and unreliable. If we start to let the child down, we risk further damage, and therefore reinforcing the child's beliefs.

Identify triggers

Having an understanding of the child's early experiences can help us to identify possible triggers that can result in the child becoming overwhelmed and moving into fight, flight or freeze survival behaviours. Triggers can be obvious: for example if there is a male with a loud voice nearby, a traumatised child might instinctively link this to earlier negative experiences involving a male with a loud voice, and therefore refuse to go near them. Despite them not posing any actual threat, it is the *perceived* threat that sends the child into survival mode.

Children may be able to tell you what their 'trigger' is and why they don't feel safe in a certain situation or with a certain person; however more often this is not the case. Often triggers are subtle, and the child is not even aware of what caused the alarm. We need to become detectives at this point to enable us to understand what is going on for the child. We need to promote communication between home and school to help us to identify triggers, as well as observing and listening. It is also important to reflect on events after they have happened, looking at the whole event one piece at a time. It can be helpful to keep a record of the times a child is 'triggered' to help to identify any common elements. These triggers could be smells, sounds, anything at all, and all elements should be considered. Regular sensory audits may need to be completed to help in this process.

There are certain behaviours that may give us clues to the child's triggers, it may be that a child can only fall asleep at night with the bedroom door wide open, or perhaps they need to sit facing the classroom door so they can see who comes in and out. At times these behaviours can appear controlling, frustrating and difficult to manage, but we must keep in mind that these may be some of the things that children need in order to feel safe.

We also need to take into account our own reaction to stress and how we respond to the child; unknowingly we may be escalating situations. Consider your body language, facial expressions and tone of voice when with a child, what messages are they getting from you?

Calming and soothing

We can help children to manage their emotions by providing things that the child finds calming and soothing. There is a huge range of equipment that can be used to support a child's needs — ranging from noise-cancelling headphones, to wiggle cushions to weighted blankets or cushions. A child may find it helpful to use a fidget toy, to have regular movement breaks, or time built into each day with a key adult. Children may find it comforting to have something with them that reminds them of their key person, or something belonging to their key person. I have known children keep a key ring in their pocket, or a note from a key person, a spray of their perfume or aftershave, a hair bobble, for example. What the item is does not matter, only that it helps to soothe the child.

It can be helpful to create a 'calm box' with the child. They can fill it with items that help to soothe and calm them. Children I have supported have kept all sorts of things in their 'calm box' — for example, bubbles, fidget toys, stress balls, a yo-yo, colouring equipment, marbles, a bouncy ball, a pack of cards, a fluffy blanket, a scented soft toy, an iPod, some ear defenders. One incredible little girl kept some high heels in hers as she loved the clip-clop sound that they made.

The child could decorate the calm box, and help to identify things they would like to keep in it. This could be kept in the classroom or within the home; the child could have one box that they keep with them wherever they go. It is their box, and needs to be kept somewhere safe where others won't have access to it.

Routines

Keeping routines safe and predictable can support the child to feel secure, as they know what is coming next. Using tools such as a visual timetable, both at home and at school, setting out the plans for the day ahead can be useful, or some older children may want to use their own calendar to look at longer periods of time. For some children a 'now and next' visual board can work well, showing what the task is now, and what will come next.

Sudden changes or times of transition can be particularly difficult for some children and they need to be explained as clearly and as early as possible in order to prepare the child. Talk to the child, and explain what will happen instead. For example, if their teacher is off poorly and a substitute teacher is called in, you could explain this to the child and introduce them to the member of staff before the school day if possible. Reassure them that an adult that they have a positive relationship with will come to see them at regular intervals throughout the day.

Other needs

It is also important to take into account other considerations, for example the child's sleep needs. Are they getting too much or too little? What does their bedtime routine look like? Is it designed for calming and soothing, or is it disorganised and chaotic, leaving the child struggling to go to sleep? Maybe the child creates the chaos? Or what does their diet look like? Is the child full of sugar and fizzy drinks, which will only lead to overstimulation? Are they getting enough fresh air and exercise, time to burn off energy, move adrenaline and cortisol from within the body, express themselves freely, and for their brain to release endorphins and help them to feel good naturally. Are they spending too much time watching screens? Time and time again this has been proven to impact greatly on the brains of children, and can cause children to become seriously overstimulated. Look at the child's environment as a whole, and most importantly – be honest.

Self-regulation

We begin learning how to self-regulate when we are infants; we learn how to contain our emotions and impulses by experiencing our primary caregiver managing theirs – and ours for us. If our experience is of someone who can self-soothe, contain and manage their emotions and impulses appropriately, then we are likely to learn to do the same.

If this is not our experience, then equally this will be our model for learning to self-regulate, or not, as the case may be, and our brain develops accordingly.

We respond to events or situations we experience depending on how we interpret them, and this is based on our experiences. If we have experienced the world as an unsafe place in our early years, we may then perceive a person bumping into us accidentally as a purposeful act, because our experience is that people hurt others on purpose. Or if a person shouts, we may automatically think that they will lash out and hit us because this is what we may have experience of. We may worry that our needs will not be met, and therefore act in many different ways in order to survive and have someone meet our needs, one way or another.

We can teach children to understand their stress response, how to notice the warning signs in their body and what the warning signs are. We can then help them to learn ways of managing these stress responses, and to find some calm. There are many examples within this book.

When we are babies we need to be held, rocked, stroked, and comforted, and from these we experience rhythmic and repetitive touch. These may not have been present or consistent for the child in their early years. Tactile experiences may have been negative or missed when the child was younger, but there are many ways to revisit these hugely important developmental building blocks. Regular movement breaks can be particularly useful for some children, especially if they can be linked to tactile and repetitive activities.

Activities that encourage rhythmic movement, such as using a swing, a trampoline, skipping rope, a spacehopper, sitting on a rocking chair, listening to music, or dancing, can be beneficial. Within the home, children may be happy to have their hair washed by a key person, or to have their nails painted or receive a foot massage for instance. Other activities could include playing tag or playing clapping games together. For some children having their hair brushed or stroked can be calming and soothing, and help them to learn to regulate their emotions as well as learn about appropriate and nurturing touch. Please bear in mind that for some children touch is *not* appropriate, and taking the child's lead with this is essential. Activities that engage the senses are hugely important here too, and there are examples later in the book.

Children can often struggle with calm and peaceful environments as they are so alien to them and their experiences. In the past these times may have been the 'calm before the storm', when the child's levels of fear would have been at their highest, watching and waiting for the chaos to ensue. Children may cause their own 'storm' in order to avoid this period of calm.

Children learn from what the adults around them model: if we are able to demonstrate an ability to self-regulate and manage our stress, and respond to the child's distress by being calm and emotionally available, then we are modelling a positive example of self-regulation. If we are not able to do this, and we join the child in their dis-regulation, we continue the cycle.

Empathy

Being able to empathise with others helps us to feel a sense of community: to connect with others, to build meaningful relationships and to be able to relate to others. Without empathy, the world can be a very lonely place. Empathising is not a skill that we are born with, it is something that we begin to develop at around two years old, and continue to develop as we grow older and begin to understand and relate to other humans. The development of empathy is aided by being around others who show us empathy. When adults name our emotions for us, 'I can see you're angry that I won't let you have another biscuit', for example. We learn to connect with emotion, develop the language to express the emotion, and experience somebody else understanding us from our frame of reference.

But what happens if this is not our early experience, or any experience? If it is interrupted for some reason, or if the people we are learning from are not consistent or able to empathise with us? What happens if we aren't able to understand the emotions of others because we are so unsure of our own? What happens if our own feelings and emotions are so painful that we can't possibly identify and accept pain in others, as it can feel like we are holding up a mirror to ourselves?

Lack of empathy can often lead to emotionally distant children who are unable to connect with their own emotions, or the emotions of others. You may see this in children who lash out and hurt another child, but say they don't care; children who destroy something belonging to another child, and can't seem to understand why the other child might be upset by this; or children who may say the most hurtful things to another child, and react with scorn when they cry.

Understanding the impact of behaviour

Children need to learn that their behaviour has an impact. It can be a challenge for adults to maintain boundaries without escalating situations further, damaging relationships, and evoking shame. Adults need to separate the child from the behaviour and avoid language such as 'You always do this', or 'You are so ungrateful', for example. Using language that talks about the behaviour as the unacceptable thing, and not the child, can help children to reflect without shame. Using 'I' statements 'when you ... I feel ...' can be useful. This reflection needs to be paired with empathy, and a calm, curious approach. Avoid shaming children in public, this can be hugely damaging to a child with an already fragile sense of self. Children need to be able to recognise any consequences as logical, and in keeping with the action. Implement any consequences as soon as possible after the incident, not carried over to the following day. The child needs the opportunity to make amends and move on from this with you, ultimately maintaining the relationship. I'm not saying it will be easy, but it will be worth it.

In summary:

- Undertake a sensory audit.
- Understand early experiences.
- Identify triggers.
- Provide soothing and calming stimuli within the environment.
- Keep boundaries and routines consistent to help children feel safe and secure.
- Identify a key person at home and one at school or anywhere else the child spends time. Our brains learn through repetition. Parents, carers and school staff are best placed to be able to offer these consistent, stable and key relationships.
- Prepare the child for changes in advance and pay attention to times of transition.
- Promote activities that include rhythmic and repetitive movement, as well as tactile experiences and ways for the child to express their emotions and communicate need.
- Model emotional containment, regulation and an ability to self-soothe when feeling overwhelmed, particularly if it is the child's behaviour that we are struggling with.
- Help children to develop the language of emotion.
- Help them by noticing the emotion and the need behind the behaviour and emotion, and name them to the child.
- Explore this need, the emotion and the behaviour, in order to help the child to understand and make links to this.
- Help children to reflect on their behaviour without triggering a shame response.

- Consider the developmental age that the child may be functioning from.
- Most importantly (in my opinion) try to provide the 'secure' base they have missed out on, be consistent, reliable, warm, caring, available, responsive, empathic and 'tuned in' to the child – and never give up. It is never too late.

Sounds like an easy task then ...

3. My back pack

Negative cycle

Often children develop self-destructive coping behaviours as they:

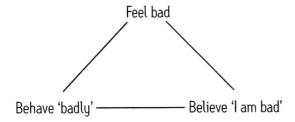

Which can become a negative cycle.

The following activities can help children to learn new coping skills or ways of managing how they feel. By learning coping strategies children can learn to manage emotions, and change the way they behave and how they think about themselves. This can then become a much more positive cycle.

My back pack

We can help a child to build up their skills, knowledge and coping strategies by encouraging them to fill up their 'back pack' with activities they're drawn to. This can help the child to feel empowered and ready to face difficulties, it can help them to manage big feelings and difficult situations, and in turn help build resilience and their confidence in themselves as well as develop their own abilities to manage.

Demonstrating the use of these techniques when you yourself are feeling overwhelmed can help to reinforce their usefulness and encourage children to try the skills for themselves. The back pack on the next page can be filled with ideas from this book and suggestions from the child to help them to feel safe and calm.

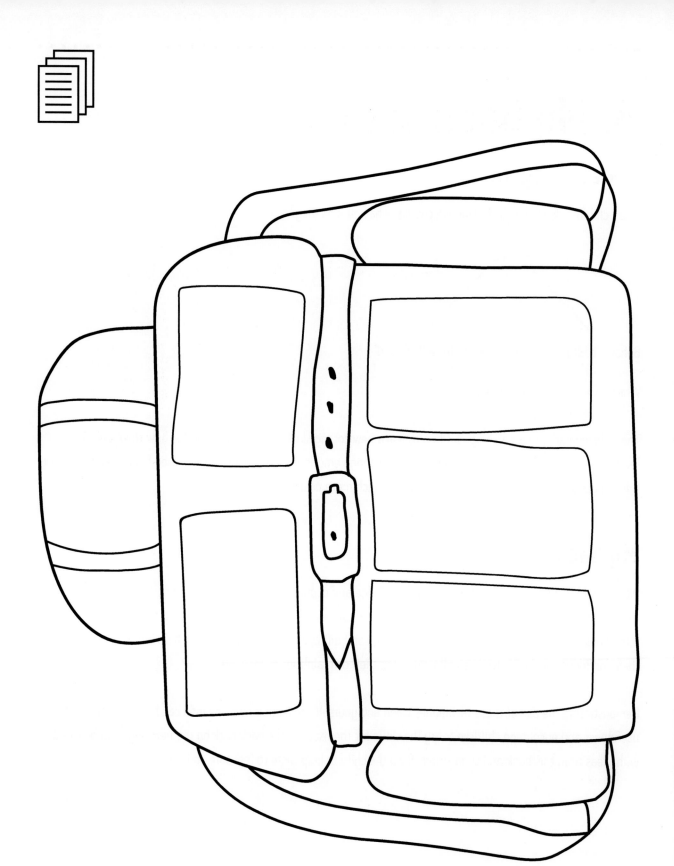

4. Brain education

It can be helpful for children to understand why they might act in a certain way particularly when it comes to feeling overwhelmed. This information needs to be delivered at a level that the child can understand, and is likely to need to be repeated many times to help the child to really understand the concept fully.

Puppets or figures can be useful to help to explain the different parts of the brain to children, and can help them to remember what you have said. One puppet or figure could represent the 'thinking' brain (the part of the brain that thinks things through logically before making decisions and acting on them), and the other puppet or figure could represent the impulsive part of the brain, the 'cave' or reptilian part (the part that does things without thinking in order to survive, or so it seems). This is also the oldest part of the brain, hence why it is often referred to as the 'reptilian' brain. You can use your own names for the parts of the brain to help the child understand the concept.

You could use any puppets or figures you like. I often find it useful to use a child or human puppet to represent the 'thinking' brain – to represent the 'real' them, the brain that thinks and acts how they would like it to when they are feeling calm. I also often use a crocodile or other reptile to represent the 'cave' or 'reptilian' brain.

Explain to the child that thousands of years ago there were cavemen and women living on Earth. They would go out hunting to find food to eat. Imagine that at the same time there was a hungry sabre-toothed tiger looking for food too, and it spots the tasty-looking caveman.

The caveman sees the danger and the 'worry alarm' inside him starts to work. When this happens the 'cave' brain takes over from the 'thinking' part of the brain.

The 'cave' brain sends signals to the body to say that to help the caveman stay alive he needs to do one three things. Fight the animal (*fight*), run away (this is also called *flight*), or stay very still and hope he hasn't been spotted (*freeze*). Doing one of these would hopefully help him to survive and escape from the sabre-toothed tiger.

We don't have sabre-toothed tigers nowadays, but sometimes we will come across other dangers.

However this part of the brain can also get it wrong, and tell us we are in danger even when we aren't. If our 'cave' brain gives us a wrong signal, a little like a 'false alarm', it can make us panic and feel like we are in danger even if we aren't. Use the puppets or figures as you are talking to link the visual 'brain' to the information you are sharing.

You can use the puppets to talk to the child about how they might respond in different situations when the 'false alarm' goes off. See if the child can suggest some scenarios, but you may have to start off the suggestions until they get the hang of it. You could talk about how the brain might react if someone pushed the child: the 'thinking' brain might want to go to tell a teacher, but the 'cave' brain might want to push the other person back or want to run away. At this point it might be useful to keep suggestions quite general, and not talk about actual events that have involved the child – keeping the conversation safe.

Explain that when we use our 'cave' brain, we might make choices and do things that we wouldn't normally do if we were using our 'thinking' brain. Sometimes the things we do when we are using our 'cave' brain can mean that we get ourselves into trouble, or do something that we feel bad about and regret afterwards.

At this point the child might feel safe enough to be able to give some examples of things that they might have done when using their 'cave' brain. You could then talk together about how they might have behaved differently if they had used their 'thinking' brain. You could also share something about times when you have used your 'cave' brain – what happened, and the consequences. The child might be able to suggest what you could have done if you had used your 'thinking' brain. Ensure that this is nothing too serious, but sharing your experiences can sometimes help children to feel safe sharing theirs and to understand that we can all be overtaken by our 'cave' brain at times.

Talk to the child about the changes in the body when the 'cave' brain takes over, which means that we might feel;

- Sweaty or shaky.
- Our mouth becomes dry.
- Our muscles become tense and tight.
- Like we have butterflies in our tummy.
- Sick.
- Our heart beats faster.
- Our head begins to ache.
- We breathe faster and more heavily.

Talking to the child about these things can let us and others know that we are in our 'cave' brain; they are clues to how we are feeling. When this happens, it is important that we get back from our 'cave' brain into our thinking brain again. We can do this by:

- Practising the breathing exercises in this book.
- Practising mindfulness.
- Using the calm-down activities in this book – or any others you can think of.
- Asking for help and talking about your feelings.

'I just hit people sometimes, and I don't know why, and then I feel so sad.' – 8-year-old boy

5. Communication and calming

Communication

Using positive language rather than negative can have a huge impact on a child's ability to follow instructions. Tell a child what you would like them to do, rather than what you don't want them to do. For example, 'don't run' then becomes 'walk' or 'stop shouting' becomes 'quiet voice'. I am not saying it will work miracles, but giving the child an instruction about 'what to do' and not 'what *not* to do' can help them to process this more quickly and be clear about what is expected. If I said to you 'stop thinking about a green elephant, stop it, stop thinking about that green elephant, don't think about it', I can guarantee your mind is seeing the green elephant. It is not recognising the 'don't' or 'stop' in the instruction and just keeps on doing it. If I changed it to 'think of an orange elephant', notice what happens.

Keeping instructions short, simple and to the point can also be helpful. Once we start to lecture, children will often zone out and miss the important parts. Say what needs to be said in as few words as possible, and check the child understands. Setting expectations does not need to have a monologue attached – as well as the child zoning out, it can leave you feeling frustrated and annoyed. For example:

'I don't know how many times I have told you, I am sick of you not picking up your towels off the bathroom floor. Every day I find a wet towel on the floor again, and it is not my job to pick up after you, you treat this place like a hotel, and I am sick of it.' Can become: 'Towels', said in a direct, calm and confident manner. If the child does not understand this, then pointing to the offending towel while saying 'Towels' or 'towels need to be hung up' is more than enough. It is a positive instruction telling them what needs to be done. They know your expectations, you have told them this many, many times before, and the child does not need to have them repeated again. The short instructions help to avoid arguments as well as avoid overexaggerating: 'I do EVERYTHING in this house, and you NEVER help' (possibly an exaggeration, possibly not – but not helpful either way). They also stop blame, which could cause the child to become defensive or feel a sense of shame (something that some children are unable to tolerate). You are not accusing them of anything: 'You are so lazy, you never do anything I ask', or shaming them: 'Look, the other children in the class have done it'. And you won't give yourself a headache from the nagging – *winning!*

For some children visual reminders need to be in place. It is often a good idea to break long tasks down into smaller tasks, with photographs or drawings to show things such as a morning routine before school, or the classroom end-of-day routine, or maybe a visual timetable for the day ahead in the classroom. You can make reminders and charts with moveable items using Velcro or magnets if needed.

Children may struggle to complete tasks if they are preoccupied, and they may also struggle with memory. Having a task list can be helpful. This is a step-by-step list that can be ticked off as the child completes each task, and can involve anything at all. If you print these out and laminate them, the child can use a felt pen to tick them off. The list can then be wiped clean and used again.

Side-by-side talking can be really effective for some children. This is when you are both doing an activity together and chatting at the same time. It might be, for example, washing the dishes, fishing, baking, driving in the car, or colouring in. For some children, feeling the intensity of sitting opposite someone, making eye contact and being expected to share thoughts and feelings can be too much. Side-by-side talking allows children to be engaged in an activity that can help them to feel more relaxed, more at ease, and more able to talk openly without feeling under pressure.

Spending time with the child when you actually have the time to listen to them with your full attention can be a huge thing for a child. Letting them know you are listening to them can be done very easily by using simple comments such as 'mmm hhh', 'oh', 'yes', 'uh huh', 'carry on'. This can help a child to continue to share with you, feel you are listening with genuine interest, and understand what they are telling you.

Try to avoid using the word 'why' when a child is sharing their thoughts and feelings with you. Often children can feel that 'why' is a judgement or an accusation, which can leave the child feeling ashamed or challenged. Children sometimes don't know 'why' they did something, or 'why' they feel the way they do.

Helpful phrases to help calm a child

There is a saying 'never in the history of calming down has anyone ever calmed down by being told to calm down' – and there is certainly some truth in this. When a child is feeling overwhelmed and in their 'cave' brain they are not able to process information. This is not the time to give lectures, tell them off, tell them the consequences, or make threats to take away toys or treats. This will only escalate the situation. Below are some examples to help to soothe a child try one of these instead. Then once the child is calm you can both talk together about what happened:

- 'How big is your worry/anger?'
  Asking the child to give you an example of how big it feels to them right now can help you to get a sense of the child's perspective. It can also be helpful as they calm down to ask them if it feels like it has shrunk in size.

- 'I am here, you are safe.'
  When children are feeling out of control they can feel unsafe and scared. Offering them comfort and reminding them that they are safe can help to reassure them.

- 'Can you draw it/write it?'
  Asking the child to express their feeling creatively can be helpful, especially if they're struggling to share them in words.

- 'What do you want to say to your feelings?'
  Asking the child to speak directly to their feelings can help to empower them, and give them some control back over those feelings.

- 'Tell me about it – tell me what is going on for you.'
  Let the child talk about how they are feeling in the present, without arguing with them, talking back or disagreeing. Sometimes for children it is enough to feel heard.

- 'What shall we use from your back pack?'
  Ask the child to pick one item – however, if they are unable to because they are so overwhelmed by their feelings, choose one for them, or perhaps ask them to breathe with you.

- 'This feeling will pass.'
  Reassure them that, with time, this feeling will pass and they will feel calm again.

- 'What do you need from me, can I help?'
  Ask them what they need from you – ask if they can think of anything that you can do to help them to feel calmer.

6. Breathing

Children can learn to calm their body and mind, self-soothe, and manage difficult emotions and sensations simply through breathing and taking note of the breath. Deep breathing can help us to calm our body and mind, reduce the stress hormone cortisol, slow our breathing rate, and decrease our heart rate. Encouraging children to slow their breath can help them when big emotions threaten to overwhelm them.

When teaching children how to breathe deeply, be aware that children often raise their shoulders up towards their ears as they take a breath. This can result in the child feeling tense, and is counterproductive to these exercises. Remind them to relax their shoulders, you could get them to lower them and give them a little wiggle to help them relax.

As with any new skill, practice makes perfect. The more the children can practise these techniques when they are feeling calm, the more comfortable they will feel about using them – and the more likely they will be to use them when they begin to feel overwhelmed.

We can teach children to use techniques that they can add to their own individual 'back pack' and access whenever they need to.

Tuning in

Tuning in to our breathing can be a clue to help us to identify how we are feeling-and help us to calm down if we are feeling overwhelmed. Talk to the child about different types of breathing – fast, slow, deep or shallow, for instance. You could ask the child if they can think with you about how a person who is breathing in a certain way might be feeling. For example, someone who feels calm and relaxed might breathe deeply and slowly. If someone is scared they might breathe quickly, taking shallow breaths.

You could practise the different types of breathing together, and discuss how it feels to breathe in different ways.

In and out

You will need: optional cupcake or flower, and bubbles.

Ask the child to imagine that they are holding a flower or a cupcake in one hand, and a bubble wand in the other hand. '*Breathe in through your nose as if you are smelling a beautiful flower, or a delicious-looking cake, and then breathe out through your mouth like you are gently blowing bubbles.*' Ask the child to really take in the smell of the flower or cupcake when they breathe in, and to really concentrate on blowing as many bubbles as they can when they let the air out. To start this off you could actually use a real flower, cupcake or bubble wand. After practice with props you can then ask the child to try without the props so that they get used to being able to use this technique whenever or wherever they need to.

Breathing ball

You will need: Hoberman's sphere, or a balloon. Please note if using balloons with children do not leave them unsupervised at any point.

A balloon or a Hoberman's sphere can be used to demonstrate to children how to breathe slowly, calmly and deeply. You can use the sphere by opening it out slowly as you breathe in and fill your lungs, and then collapse it again when you breathe out slowly. This helps to demonstrate the filling and emptying of your lungs as you breathe in and out. It can also help children to practise breathing in and out slowly, as they can use the ball as a visual cue for how slowly to breathe.

You can also use this technique to demonstrate what breathing looks like when people are upset and stressed, and not breathing properly, by demonstrating fast, shallow breathing with the sphere.

You could then use this to help children to understand that when we do not breathe correctly, panic messages are sent to the brain telling us that we are not OK. Equally, breathing calmly can send a more positive message to the brain to say that things are OK, and we are safe

Breathing aids

It can be helpful to give children a small printout as a visual aid to keep in a pocket. The printout could be laminated or put on card to make it last longer. Doing this can help children to follow certain instructions until they are able to remember the techniques on their own. Instructions could also be printed out and put on the child's bedroom wall, the fridge, the classroom wall, or anywhere else you and the child feel may be helpful.

Counting slowly, breathe in through your nose
and out through your mouth for the count of:

in 1 out 1	in 2 out 2
in 3 out 3	in 4 out 4
in 5 out 5	in 6 out 6

Another suggestion is to ask the child to trace a special shape slowly with their fingers, following the guide of when to breathe in and when to breathe out. This can help children to regulate their breathing and find calm.

You can use any shape (please see the example below), and this is likely to be all the more successful if it is a shape that the child has chosen themselves.

You could show the child how to do this using their own hand. This means that they don't need to rely on using a prompt, or standing out and possibly having other people notice. After all, they will always have their hand with them: it's more discreet and they can use this technique anywhere. If the child has a close, trusted adult it may be appropriate for them to trace the adult's hand with their finger: when they trace up a finger they breathe in slowly, and when they trace down the other side they breathe out slowly. They can repeat this as many times as they like.

If the child struggles to trace their own finger slowly enough the adult could use their own finger to slowly trace the child's hand. The touch can have a calming element for the child alongside the slow breathing. The hope would be that the child would learn to do this for themselves eventually, so I would recommend agreeing that you will only trace their hand once or twice each time they use this technique, and agree that the child then takes over. Please keep in mind that this touch might not be appropriate for all children.

Breathing tools

You will need: art materials such as ribbons, tissue paper and feathers, paper or plastic cup, toilet roll tube, pipe cleaners.

Making breathing tools can help children to see their breath as they practise and make it a fun way of connecting with their breath. There are many ways of doing this. I have suggested below a few that children usually enjoy making.

You can use a paper or plastic cup with a hole in the base to make a great breathing tool. The child can decorate it by attaching ribbons, feathers, or bits of paper or string around the rim of the cup, which will then move as the child breathes into it.

An empty toilet roll tube can be decorated using tissue paper or other light art materials. Children can decorate the tube, and practise breathing in different ways through it.

A pipe cleaner can be used as a make-believe bubble wand. Fold it in half and leave a section for a loop at the top, then twist the rest together. They can use it to blow real bubbles using a bubble mixture or washing-up liquid, or can just use the bubble wand/pipe cleaner to blow imaginary bubbles.

Blowing bubbles

You will need: bubble mixture and bubble wand.

Using bubbles and a bubble wand, you can give the child an opportunity to 'blow away' a worry or feeling they would like to 'get rid of' with each bubble they blow. They can share the worry or feeling with you, and then blow them away, real or imagined. The child can watch the worry or feeling float away and pop, or they could pop the bubbles themselves. This can encourage the child to focus on their breath in order to form the bubbles – if they blow too gently the bubble won't form, and if the breath is too heavy then it will pop before it forms correctly. This can help the child to regulate their breath and it can also be cathartic as the child is 'getting rid of' certain feelings by expressing them.

Visual breathing

Ask the child to lie down somewhere comfortable. They could choose a teddy bear, a bean bag or a sticker for this exercise. Explain that having the item on their tummy will help them to see their breath. The aim is for them to move the object up and down with the breath without it falling off. This can help to encourage slow and steady breathing and relaxation.

Warm and cool

Experimenting with breathing can help children to feel interested, and keen to learn. Ask the child to put their hand by their mouth and notice the difference in temperature between the 'in' breath (cool), and the 'out' breath (warm). Children often find it fascinating that when we make a 'haaa' sound (as if we are steaming up a window) the breath feels warm, and if you make a 'hooo' sound (as if you are cooling down a hot drink) the breath feels cooler.

You could also use this as an opportunity to talk to the child about what happens to their breath in their body.

Ava breathing

Show the child how to stand up straight with their feet wide apart. Explain to the child you are both going to pretend to be Ava the elephant from the story. Pretend that your arms are your long, grey trunk. Start off by dangling your trunk in front of you. As you breathe in through your nose lift your trunk up high in the air like an elephant trumpeting. When you breathe out again bring your trunk back down to dangle and swing in front of you again. Repeat this several times.

7. Mindfulness

Mindfulness is focusing on what is happening inside and around you at a precise moment. It is not trying to change what is happening, but just being aware of it, compassionate towards it, and 'tuned in'. It is an opportunity to stop for a few minutes, and just 'be' in the moment. It allows us to stop and actually be 'present' and consciously with the child in the moment.

Children are often present. For most children it is a relatively natural state for them to adopt. However, when children have had difficult experiences, they can struggle to access this state as naturally as other children because of their need to be 'hyper-vigilant' and alert to danger at all times – which means looking outwards and not inwards. A child's thoughts can often race ahead as a safety precaution, and children can become disconnected from their feelings and bodily sensations.

Mindfulness can be an opportunity to help children to slow down, and begin to tune in to their body. The more they can practise this, the more the children can develop the ability to do this themselves, and learn to use these techniques when they experience overwhelming feelings.

Mindfulness can help children to learn that all feelings will come *and* go – and all will pass eventually. It is important for children to learn that they don't have to fight their feelings, push them away, change them, be scared of them, or ignore them.

There are many ways to help support children to use mindfulness throughout their day. Leading by example can be very powerful, and children learn from what they see. Being mindful can also help with your own self-care too – *win, win!*

Mindfulness can:

- help to promote positive mood and self-esteem;
- help to improve mental health, by reducing depression and anxiety;
- help children to improve concentration and focus on learning;
- help to reduce aggression;
- help to promote positive behaviour, emotional control, empathy and emotional intelligence.

'We practise mindfulness as a whole class. It has really helped a lot of the children, and makes the class a calmer place. It means that when individual children need to use the techniques they don't stand out, and the other children carry on with their work.' – Primary school teacher

Mindfulness exercises

Right now

Check in with the child and ask them what is going on inside them right now. How does their body feel: are they hot, cold, warm? Do they feel calm and relaxed or excited? Encourage children to 'check in' with themselves regularly, and they will hopefully become used to doing this. Repetition is the key to helping children learn a new way of approaching things.

Jumble jar

You will need: A jar or see-through bottle (I would suggest using a plastic container for safety reasons), glitter, sparkly bits, water, glue.

For this exercise you will need to make a jumble jar to use. You can make it before the session, or you can make it with the child. I find that children enjoy the making itself, and it helps them to really engage in the later part of the activity.

Ask the child to put glitter in the bottom of the container. They can also add other sparkly bits and pieces if they want to. Fill the jar with water, and, once the child is happy with their concoction, seal it with the lid. I would advise that you glue the lid on to avoid spillages or curious children opening it up.

Explain to the child that the jumble jar represents our mind and body and the glitter represents our thoughts and emotions. Shake the jumble jar up and down to unsettle the glitter and make it swirl. As you are doing this, tell the child that this is sometimes how our mind and body feel when we have lots of thoughts or emotions swirling around, and it's no wonder we find it hard to think straight with all of that going on. Ask the child to sit quietly and take some calm breaths as they watch the water and glitter start to slow down, and begin to float gently down and settle. Explain to the child that this is how we can bring ourselves back to being calm – by breathing calmly, and taking a few moments to relax. We can think so much more clearly when we are calm. It is also a great opportunity to explain to children that all feelings pass, and even when they feel like the jumble jar, they will feel calm again soon.

Mindful sensory walk

Invite the child to take part in a mindful sensory walk. This can be done inside or outside, at home or at school, anywhere at all. As you walk, ask the child to be aware of what they can see, hear, smell, feel and even taste.

Ask them to do this in silence (or spend some of the time in silence if this is difficult for the child) so they can be fully aware of their senses, and what they are experiencing in the here and now. Take your time with this, and, dependent on a child's ability to stay with this, it may be something you build up over time.

You could choose just one of the senses to focus on during each walk. You could talk to the child about the senses of the body, and ask them to choose which of the senses to focus on that day. Then really concentrate on that sense as you walk. 'Did you hear that sound?', 'I wonder what made that sound', 'I can hear a car, do you hear it?'

To further this exercise you could ask the child to create a picture of their experience to help them to reflect fully. They could do this using a variety of art materials, and could also represent their experience using colours, shapes and symbols.

Mindful colouring

You will need: colouring sheets/books, pens, pencils or crayons.

Mindful colouring can help relieve stress and promote relaxation. It can help people enter an almost meditative state through the repetitive action of the colouring. It can help children to focus on the task at hand, introducing mindfulness, and help calm negative thoughts and emotions.

You could use this picture of Ava to help introduce children to mindful colouring.

8. Relaxation

You will need: a comfortable place to sit or lie, blankets and cushions are optional.

You could start by using the following script to explain to children why relaxation is important.

Relaxation is a very important way for us to learn to manage and cope with big feelings. Feeling relaxed can help us to cope much better with stress. It can help us to feel less tired and tense, and can help us to focus and concentrate better. Relaxation skills can also help us to sleep better and feel more confident.

Below are some ideas and examples of how to practise relaxation. Why not try them out, and choose one you like and practise it? Why not add it to your 'back pack'?

Magic carpet ride

We are going to use our imagination now. We are going to practise using our imagination to help us to relax, and feel good. The more we practise using our imagination in this way, the easier it becomes – a bit like lifting weights at the gym, where our muscles get bigger and stronger and it gets easier to lift the weight, the same happens with our imagination: the more we use it, the bigger and stronger it becomes, and the easier it is to use.

First of all, get in a comfortable position, this might be lying down, or sitting comfortably. Now, I am going to ask you to close your eyes, and take a deep breath in ... and out ... breathe in ... and out ... keep concentrating on breathing in and out slowly and deeply.

We are going to imagine that we are going on a wonderful journey, a journey you are feeling very excited about. We are going on a magic carpet ride. Picture your magic carpet on the floor in front of you. What colour is it? Is it bright and multi-coloured, or is it just one colour; does it have tassels and ribbons coming from it? Is there a cushion for you to sit on?

Now step onto your magic carpet gently, make yourself comfortable, feel how soft the carpet is. When you are ready, tap the carpet gently, and in your head say the magic words 'high in the sky'. Feel the carpet gently lift off the ground and begin to move forwards out of the door and up, up into the sky.

Look around you, what can you see? Can you see the cars and trees below getting smaller as the carpet takes you up into the bright, blue sky? See the people below waving at you from the ground. Look how tiny they look from all the way up here.

Notice the clouds as you pass, can you reach out and touch one, feel your hand move through it gently.

Notice the birds flying alongside you as you fly on your magic carpet. Are they pigeons, eagles or maybe even brightly coloured parrots? Hear them tweeting and singing to you as they fly beside you.

You are moving away from the town now, and ahead you can see the deep, blue sea. It sparkles like a million diamonds with the bright, yellow sun shining on it. Feel the warm sunshine on your skin and face as you move towards the sea.

You can smell the salt in the air and the seaweed below as you look down and see the yellow, sandy beach. As the carpet takes you across the sea you look down and see dolphins swimming through the waves, jumping out of the water to say hello. You follow the dolphins as they swim further out to sea.

The sun is starting to go down, it will be dark soon, and it's time to go home. The carpet turns back to-wards the land, moving gently back across the sea, heading for the beach. It moves slowly back across the town and, as you see your house in the distance, the carpet starts to bring you slowly towards the ground. It touches down on the ground just outside the front door.

You climb off your magic carpet, bend down and roll it up, and carry it into the house and put it somewhere safe. You know that you can use your magic carpet to go on another journey any time you like. Where might you go next time? Into space, the mountains, the jungle, anywhere your imagination can take you.

Your space

This is a guided visualisation to use with children to help them to relax and to find calm spaces within their minds. The aim is to practise this with the child to help them to be able to eventually access their 'space' whenever they need to feel calm and relaxed.

You can use the following script, but please feel free to adapt it however you see fit.

We are going to practise imagining a safe place, a place that is just for you This is called 'your space'. This is something you can do, somewhere you can go in your mind when you're feeling sad, worried, scared or angry. You can do this whenever you like, whenever you want to feel more relaxed and calm. The more you practise this, the easier it will be to go to your space whenever you need to.

Sit or lie down, making sure you are comfortable. This works best with your eyes closed, but if you don't feel you can do that just yet, that's OK – you might feel like you can close your eyes later.

Take a deep, slow breath in through your nose, and let it out slowly from your mouth. Keep breathing in and out slowly, and as you do this feel your body start to relax.

Now start to imagine a place where you feel calm and safe, it could be a real place, or it could be a make-believe or imaginary place. It could be in a field full of flowers, or maybe floating through space. It doesn't matter where it is, as long as you feel calm and relaxed when you think of yourself there.

Look around 'your space' slowly, what can you see? What is in and around 'your space'? Is it dark or light?

What can you feel in 'your space'? Can you feel the cool wind or the sunshine on your face? Are you sitting on something soft, like sand on a beach, or a hard piece of rock at the top of a mountain?

What can you hear in 'your space'? Are there any noises around you?

What can you smell in 'your space'?

What can you taste on your tongue?

Keep taking deep breaths as you look around 'your space'; notice how calm and relaxed you feel when you are in 'your space'. This is your special place, you can come here in your mind whenever you need to feel more relaxed and calm, and you can stay here as long as you like.

Sometimes your adults might ask if you need some time out to go to 'your space' if they can see that you might need some calm time. When you are ready, take another deep breath, start to wiggle your fingers and toes, and slowly open your eyes again coming back from 'your space' into the room.

As an extension activity you can ask the child to draw or paint their space on paper. They could draw it as an actual space as they saw it, or you could ask them to create it using colours and shapes to show how they feel when they are in their space. The art they create can be used as a visual reminder that they can access their space whenever they need to, and can also help to reinforce and even enhance their space, cementing it further in their imagination. This can make it easier for them to see it in detail and also to return to it in their mind.

Muscle relaxation

Teaching children the skill of being able to relax their body is a lifelong skill that they can use wherever and whenever they feel tense. This exercise can be done as quickly or as slowly as you like – use your judgement and knowledge of the child. Consider how long you feel they can focus for, and take it from there. Start small, and build it up.

Muscles can be grouped together to make the exercise shorter, or you can ask the child to focus on one muscle at a time to make it longer. It really doesn't matter how you do it, just that the child is able to learn to focus on and isolate their muscles, and then learn to notice the difference between a tense muscle and a relaxed one. Once they have practised this technique, it is something they can use in the classroom if they are feeling tense, or on the football pitch or when playing on their games console, and hopefully, later on in life, at work or on the bus. Some people find this helps them to get to sleep at night.

Once the child knows how to do it, they can do it without closing their eyes and being talked through it. This makes it a skill the child can use anywhere at any time, and no one else will even notice. It is best to get the child to practise this when they are not feeling particularly tense or anxious. They will be able to engage more positively with it, and will be more likely to use it when they are actually feeling tense.

When they are more familiar with this technique, you can randomly call out a muscle or muscle group for them to isolate and tense/relax during the day, again strengthening their ability to do this and to remind them of their ability to relax their body.

Lie or sit in a comfortable position, close your eyes if you can, and let your body go floppy and loose. Take some deep, slow breaths in and out to help you to relax. Notice your breathing, in .... and out ... in ... and out. We are going to practise helping your body to relax by squeezing and tensing your muscles for a few seconds, and then relaxing them. We will start with your feet and move up to your head.

Let's start with your feet. Curl your toes tightly, squeezing them, keep squeezing for 5, 4, 3, 2, 1, and relax, notice the difference you can feel between the tensing feeling and how your feet feel now.

Take some more deep breaths in ... and out ... in ... and out.

Now let's move up to your calves, the bottom part of your legs. Lift your toes up towards the sky, this will make your calf muscles tight. Stay like this for 5, 4, 3, 2, 1, and relax.

Take some more deep breaths in ... and out ... in ... and out.

Now your thighs, the tops of your legs, squeeze your thighs together tightly for 5, 4, 3, 2, 1, and relax.

Let's take some more deep breaths in ... and out ... in ... and out.

Now onto your tummy. Suck your tummy in and hold it for 5, 4, 3, 2, 1, and relax.

Take some more deep breaths in ... and out ... in ... and out.

Up to your chest now, take a deep breath in and hold it for 5, 4, 3, 2, 1, and relax.

Go back to taking some more deep breaths in ... and out ... in ... and out.

Now onto your shoulders and neck, squeeze your shoulders up towards your ears, and hold it like that for 5, 4, 3, 2, 1, and relax.

Take some deep breaths, in ... and out ... in and out. Notice the difference now that your shoulders and neck at more relaxed, notice how loose they feel now, and how you have dropped them down low.

Now this bit might seem a bit strange, I want you to squeeze your face into the funniest looking scrunched up face you can manage, that's it, your mouth, nose and forehead, and hold it there for 5, 4, 3, 2, 1, and relax.

Take some more slow, deep breaths now, in ... and out ... in ... and out. Notice how relaxed and floppy your body feels now. You can use this whenever you like, when you feel your muscles becoming tense and stiff. You can do your whole body one part at a time, or just choose a part of your body. You might feel your shoulders are getting stiff and tense, and might just decide to lift them up and squeeze and hold for a few seconds, and then relax them. Or maybe you are clenching your jaw or your fists tightly, and want to relax them. You can use this however you like, whenever you like, and the best part about it is that no one has to even know you are doing it, it's like having a secret relaxation weapon.

Ava's trunk stretch

Ask the child to sit on the floor with their legs out straight in front of them. Explain that you are both going to pretend to be an elephant, just like Ava in the story.

You can sit with the child to demonstrate. Show the child how to stretch their arms forwards towards their toes. Pretend your arms are the elephant's trunk, and as you bend forwards blow air out and reach. See how far you can reach with your trunk, and next time see if you can reach a little further.

9. Senses and making connections

Children who have suffered trauma may have missed out on some of the experiences that promote healthy development of the brain. Encouraging children to connect with their body through their senses can strengthen their self-awareness and help them to connect to the world around them using their senses. It can also help children to develop their ability to self-regulate and recognise their body's feedback.

Sensory work can be calming for children, but for some it can become overwhelming. If you notice a child becoming uncomfortable in any way you may need to stop the activity and do an activity that helps them to feel calm again.

By focusing on one sense at a time, children can experience tuning into that particular sense. There are many different ways of doing this, below are some suggestions:

Sound

Musical instruments are a fun way to explore sound with children, but pots and pans can work too. Letting children express themselves freely through music can also be therapeutic, maybe not for your ears however! You could help children to create their own musical instruments, for example, a home-made rain stick (you can find out how to make one online), a guitar made from elastic bands stretched over a pan, a water xylophone using glasses filled with different amounts of water, or a home-made shaker made using rice and a container. There are so many items that you can find around the house or school that can be used as instruments. You could take the child on a 'sound hunt' checking to see what sounds things around you make.

You could fill plastic containers with items like marbles, coins, pasta, salt, or nuts and bolts. They can be used as shakers. Or you could make two of each and the children could try to match the same sounds together. You can encourage the child to explore the different jars, by asking questions: 'Is one is louder?', 'Are some quieter than others?', 'Do the sounds remind you of anything?'

Touch

Creating a textile bag or box can encourage a sensory connection through touch. It can encourage the child to pay attention, be curious and take risks.

You can put various objects into a box or a bag and encourage the child to put their hand in to try to work out what the objects are by touching them. You could also ask the child to describe the object to you by telling you what it feels like, for example 'it is smooth' or 'it feels heavy'.

Alternatively you could put different textured materials into trays for the child to touch with their hands or with their bare feet. Suggestions include sand, water, tin foil, a blanket, bubble wrap, washing-up liquid, corrugated cardboard – the list is endless. You could ask the child to notice and describe the different sensations when touching the materials. You might ask them if they prefer one over the others, or really don't like the feeling of another, and the reasons for this.

You could create a sensory board for children that can help to soothe and calm them, and they could keep it with them. These can be made to any size or shape, and you can use any materials you like to fix onto the board. For example, you could use pom-poms, marbles, sponges, plastic, lines of pipe cleaners, or any other items you may have.

Children could make their own 'squish balls' from balloons filled with rice or flour. I like to put a few balloons inside each other to strengthen the 'squish balls'.

Weighted cushions can easily be made, as can weighted soft toys. Some children can feel a sense of calm when they have a weighted object on their lap. It can calm feelings of anxiety and stress. You could remove the stuffing from a soft toy or the inner filling from a cushion and refill with rice. Be careful not to overfill the items: leave some room for the rice to move around inside. And also ensure you don't make the item too heavy, just heavy enough for the child to feel the effect.

Sight

'I-spy' can be a good way to encourage children to focus on sight. It can be fun, and it's a game that can be played with children at various developmental ages. If the child struggles with letters, they could use sounds to identify the object, for example the 'C' for 'Chair' can become 'ch' for 'chair' instead. In order to avoid letters altogether you could identify items using colour, for example: 'I spy with my little eye something the colour of ...'

Making a sensory bottle for sight can be done using water and adding in various small objects. You can then ask children to spot certain objects in the bottle; you can also try making bottles filled only with objects of a certain colour, adding food colouring in the same colour.

Taste

Exploring taste can be fun for children, and there you can use many things you already have in the kitchen. Sugar, salt, lemon, fruit, parmesan cheese, chocolate, salted crisps are just some examples that can be used for children to explore taste. Ask them to describe what they notice about the taste, not just what the item is, but is it sweet, salty, bitter or sour? Children often enjoy using jelly beans to identify flavours too.

Smell

To engage a child's sense of smell, you could use many items. Strong scents work best as they can be easily noticed and can help children develop an interest in the activity. Once the child becomes more in tune with their sense of smell you can then move on to less obvious scents.

Orange segments, lemon peel, lavender, spices and herbs are just some examples. Ask the child to close their eyes (if they feel comfortable doing this) and breathe in the smell. Explore with them which they like and any they don't like. Ask 'Can you describe how it smells?'

You could play a 'guess the smell' game. Children often enjoy making their own 'smell potion', mixing a variety of different smelling items into a mixing bowl to experiment with mixing and creating new smells.

Feeling senses

You may wish to ask children to describe various emotions in terms of their sensory experiences, for example asking 'What does ... look like? Sound like? Taste like? Smell like? Feel like?'

For example:

Happiness
Looks like flowers
Sounds like the ice cream van
Tastes like ice cream
Smells like sun cream
Feels like a warm blanket

Quick sense

Try the following exercises for quick sensory experiences.

• Take a deep breath in, fill your cheeks full of air as if you are going underwater, and hold it for six seconds, then slowly let it out.
• Poke your tongue out of your mouth and quickly pull it back in again, like you are sticking your tongue out at someone and don't want them to see. Repeat this.

- Stretch your arms up high and stand with your legs apart. Stretch as far as you can reach with your arms and legs out wide, like a star in the sky.
- Tense up your whole body from the top of your head to the tips of your toes, hold this for five seconds, and then relax your whole body like a rag doll.
- Hold your hands out in front of you and imagine each finger is a candle; blow out each candle one at a time.
- Cross your arms across your chest, touching your shoulders, and squeeze, giving yourself a big, warm hug.

Making connections

It is important to help children to understand that when their emotions change there are also physical changes in their body.

You could begin by asking the child if they notice any changes in their body when they feel happy. Some children may be more aware of these changes than others, for some they may have never been asked to make the link and might look at you strangely, but even so they might be able to recall some changes when they consider it.

Children are often able to relate to feeling excited and may link this to a sense of having butterflies or frogs in their tummy. Others might recognise that if they are feeling sad they may cry. Talk through different emotions with the child. You might like to make some suggestions if they struggle to identify the changes in their body when they experience different emotions, 'When you are angry have you ever noticed that your heart beats like a speeding train?'

It may be that you choose to focus on one particular emotion at a time with the child, or cover a wide range, please use whichever you feel will be more effective at helping the child to begin to link emotion with physiological changes in their body.

Becoming more in tune with their body can help children to become 'emotion detectives'. The more children can become aware of their body's responses, the more able they will become at identifying their emotions, and therefore be able to respond appropriately. This can help children to stay in their 'thinking brain' as a result.

Encourage the child to tune in to their emotions regularly. It may be that a trip to the park results in excitement, so simply ask them to describe what is happening inside their body at that moment; or the child may be feeling sad, tell them that you can see they are feeling sad, and that you know that because they are crying; you could ask them if there is anything else they are aware of in their body.

10. Expressing emotion

Many children find it difficult to express themselves verbally, and, as we have already covered, this can be particularly true for children who have had difficult early experiences. There are many ways for children to express how they are feeling without having to verbalise it. I have suggested below some that I have found to have been the most successful from the work I have done with children.

While doing the activities, encourage the child to connect with their experience and how they are feeling in the moment. For example you could say 'I wonder how the water feels on your hands. Does it feel warm? Or maybe cool?' or 'I'm wondering how it feels when you mix those paints with your fingers.'

Please remember we don't always need to know and understand what is happening internally for a child – they themselves are often unaware. When we try to interpret and guess what a child might be telling us, we can often get it very wrong. The important thing is not us making sense of it; the important thing is that the child has the opportunity to express what is inside of them, and for us to simply witness this.

Water and sand

Water can be extremely relaxing and soothing – think about how soothing a bath can be. Pouring from containers, playing with toys, experimenting with objects that float or sink, or adding food colouring or glitter to the water are all ways to be creative with water. However, simply using plain water with some measuring jugs can be just as effective.

Children may not have been given the opportunity to engage in messy play, for example. These are experiences that help young children to develop and grow, and revisiting, or even visiting these experiences perhaps for the first time, can help a child's development even at this later stage.

Sand can be used dry or wet. Wet sand can be moulded and shaped more easily and can allow for building tunnels or mountains for example.

Dry sand can be used to bury items. Children often enjoy the feeling of the soft, cool sand running through their hands, and, as with water, they often find it relaxing to pour sand from one container to another. The child may like to use various figures, toys, shells or stones in the sand to tell a story or play out a scene. Allow them to stay in the metaphor and with the story they are telling.

Puppets

Hand puppets, finger puppets, sock puppets, or string puppets are all useful when helping children to express themselves. Often, for children owning their thoughts and feelings can be difficult; but sharing them can be even harder. Fear of judgement, not being clear about how they actually feel, or not having the vocabulary to express themselves are just some of the barriers children face. Encouraging a child to use puppets as a tool for expression can help them to bypass some of these barriers. Talking through a puppet allows the puppet to own the child's feelings and express them on the child's behalf, as if they were the puppets. This can help children to share difficult feelings or experiences, and feel free to say what they wish to, but may be scared to. It is vital that you stay in the metaphor with the child, and if it is the puppet sharing something, you respond as if the puppet is really sharing it, not the child.

Painting

Children often find creativity through painting a great way to express themselves. Allowing them to take control of choosing the colours, pouring them into the palettes, and choosing what kind of picture they are going to create can help them to feel a sense of control over the process. Children are often told what to paint, given the colours and amounts to use by an adult, and are not used to being trusted in this way.

The child may pour out 'too much' into the pallet, which may go against every instinct in your body relating to waste and mess. Try to resist these instincts and allow the child the autonomy to do this themselves. Comments about waste are not necessary: try to view the whole activity from start to end as an expression, not just the painting itself.

Colours and textures, and the spreading, flowing and mixing of the paints, can be extremely therapeutic for children.

You could ask the child to express a particular feeling, how they are feeling at the time of painting, or simply allow them to express themselves however they like.

Finger painting, or even using their feet to create pictures, can help children to get in touch with an earlier stage in their development as it encourages tactile experiences. It is intentionally messy and does not require the child to stay 'within the lines', or aim for any kind of perfection. For some children this freedom to express themselves messily, and without expectations, can take away the fear of failure as there is no artistic skill required. For others this freedom may be too overwhelming, and the child may need some direction, at least to begin with.

Painting doesn't have to be limited to paint. You could use different liquids or sauces found in most kitchens: tomato sauce, chocolate spread, washing up liquid, shaving foam – the list is endless. When using these household items, the child is able to experience different textures, as well as smells, and if you use only edible items, also taste.

Music

Music can help children to express themselves through movement and connect to the feelings that they experience while listening to it. Music and beats, or musical instruments that have a rhythmic, repetitive sound to them, can work well with children who have experienced trauma.

Children can suggest some music that they like to listen to; they may be able to share different songs that make them feel a range of emotions.

You could choose a variety of music to play and ask the child to move around the room showing how they feel when they hear the music. Do they move quickly, skipping around the room, or slowly and sadly plodding as they move? If the child doesn't feel confident demonstrating how they are feeling through movement, they may be able to tell you how the music makes them feel or put it down on colouring paper. It really doesn't matter how they communicate it, just that they can notice the different emotions that come with different sounds.

Some children may struggle and not be able to do this, or choose not to identify different emotions. This is OK, it may not be an activity that works for them, and it might be better to move onto something else, or simply share with the child the different feelings that *you* experience as a result of the songs or sounds. The child may then begin to join in, may begin to register their own feedback in their head, or simply benefit from experiencing someone else sharing their feelings. Play it by ear, some might even say!

Clay/play-dough

Using clay and play-dough can be a calming way for children to express their emotions. As they are soft, pliable and tactile, they can have a soothing effect and help children to connect with their senses. You can make your own play-dough with added scents and colours too.

These materials can be used with or without direction. Children who struggle with perfectionism often feel safe using clay and play-dough, as mistakes can easily be changed or corrected. For children who have experienced an insecure attachment, failure can be devastating.

Creation can be fluid, and you do not have to set out with the intention of creating anything in particular, but just see what emerges. In this way clay and play-dough can be very liberating and allow the child to be creative.

Anger can be expressed brilliantly with clay and play-dough: they can be pounded, dropped from a height, or punched and pinched.

You can provide the child with some instruments to use for cutting, sculpting, rolling, or simply let them use their hands.

Drawing feelings

Asking children to draw their feelings on paper can help them learn that expression of emotion can help to relieve overwhelming feelings. This can be particularly helpful for children who may not have the emotional vocabulary to describe their emotions. Often children are unsure how or what they are feeling, and they may find it too difficult to own their emotions by sharing them verbally. Expressing themselves through art can help the child to share, but also keep an element of privacy.

Anger can be expressed on a piece of paper through scribbling, using various colours and sharp jagged edges for example. The paper can then be crumpled up, torn up or thrown away if the child wishes. The act of throwing away emotions once they have been expressed can be healing for children, and a symbol of moving on from them, hopefully feeling calmer.

Children can be encouraged to express any feelings they like – in fact the more they can practise this with a variety of feelings, the more used to expressing themselves they may become, which should mean that, when the child is feeling overwhelmed, they are more likely to use this as a way of expressing themselves.

Stories

Stories can be a wonderful tool to use in many different ways. Reading to a child can be soothing and comforting and provide a nurturing experience. For some children, who have not experienced this in their earlier years, it can also be cathartic and healing, and help to promote positive relationships with the adult who is reading to them.

Children often enjoy the rhythm of a rhyming story, and the repetition and predictability often found within children's books.

Children can learn about feelings from stories, and they can help children to develop empathy for characters as well as explore emotions. It can be useful to select books that contain issues that you might wish to discuss with the child. Talking about the character can feel safer for the child than having to reflect on themselves.

11. Key person activities

These exercises are designed to help promote the relationship and connection between the child and their key person. They can also help to increase understanding between two people, by encouraging connections that would usually take place naturally when the child is a baby. As we know, this is not the case for some children. By revisiting these important stages, even though later on, we can support the children as they begin to build skills they may not have developed at an earlier age.

- When you see that the child is demonstrating an emotion, share it with them. This does not just have to be an emotion they are finding difficult to tolerate. It could be when you notice they are feeling excited, or maybe shy. Doing this can let the child know that you are 'tuned in' to and able to read their emotions and care enough to notice. Doing this can also help the child to increase their emotional vocabulary, becoming more able to notice and share their emotional state. Statements such as 'look at your big smile, you are feeling happy', or 'I see how angry you feel right now, your fists are clenched tightly, and so is your jaw' could be used.

- Spend time wondering, with the child, what others may be feeling. You can do this when reading books together, looking through magazines, or watching films or television. You can also do this with real people when out shopping together, or, for example, quietly ask them what they think someone might be feeling, and how they know this. You could say, for example, 'Mrs Watson looks happy. I wonder what has made her feel happy?', or 'I think Jessica is feeling excited, can you see? She is hopping around, and has a big smile on her face.' You could take this further and link an event to a feeling, for example 'When Ellie was unkind to Lauren it hurt her feelings and Lauren feels sad, can you see she is crying?' This can help the child to begin to link facial expressions with emotions and help develop their emotional language. The child may become more adept at understanding a person's feelings and better able to develop feelings of empathy. It can also be a fun 'game' for you both to play together too, building your relationship.

- Comment on how the child's actions affect others. For example, 'When you gave Thomas one of your sweets, he looked happy', or 'Alfie was very excited when you invited him to play'. This can help children to understand that their actions have consequences, and that they themselves can help others to feel positive or negative – including you, 'When we work together as a team I feel really happy and warm inside'.

- When we are busy it can often mean we spend time multi-tasking. This can sometimes result in having conversations and spending time with children without actually looking at them or making eye contact. However, when you are together, try to make a point of looking at the child, making eye contact and letting them see your face. Be careful to do this without invading the child's personal space, and if they appear to feel comfortable about being in close proximity using eye contact, respond accordingly and build this in slowly. We are naturally drawn to engaging with babies in this way, ensuring they can see our face, and we can emulate this in our interaction with a child even at this later stage. Some children may not be able to tolerate this level of connection at first, so respond to their needs and go slowly.

- Have regular 'check ins' with the child throughout the day at pre-agreed times, particularly around times of transition, which can be stressful for some children. You could make an emotional 'check in' and ask them how they are feeling at that moment. This could be done using an emotion word with a score for how they are feeling (0 could be the worst and 10 the most amazing, for example), or you could use a colour system or a weather element.

- Sit facing one another and take it in turns to choose an emotion (you could use emotion cards if you like). Take it in turns to make the face of someone experiencing this emotion, while the other person copies. You could do this activity in two ways, either where both people know what the emotion is, or where the other person has to guess. Make this decision based on the child's ability and understanding of emotions.

- Stand or sit opposite each other. Explain to the child that you are going to take turns to pretend to be a mirror. One person will make a movement and the other one (the mirror) will copy what they are doing. They will try to copy the movements at the same time, as if you are actually looking in a mirror. This can be difficult at first, and you can say that to the child, but if you both practise, it will get easier. It means trying to think about what the other person might do even before they have done it.

12. Movement breaks

Below are some suggestions of movement break activities that can be used with children wherever they are. These are simple activities to be used when a child needs a 'break' from whatever they were doing. Movement breaks can support children when they need to regulate their emotions or burn off excess energy, and help them to return to their original activity calmer and more ready to engage.

These activities can be written out on cards or paper and then laminated. They can then be put on lollipop sticks, or in jars, or on a key ring. Just ensure they're accessible, and use them accordingly. How long a child needs for an active break and how often depends entirely on what works for the child, and may be trial and error to begin with.

Use your imagination, get the child involved, and try to come up with some new and unusual ones, the more wacky and fun, usually the better for the child.

- Make big circles with your arms
- Build a tower
- Jump on the spot 10 times
- Run around the garden or playground
- Walk like ... a soldier, a duck, a horse
- Do 10 jumping jacks
- Touch your toes and hold for 5 seconds
- Play with a hula hoop
- Wiggle your body
- March with high knees around the room
- Crawl like a bear
- Kick a ball to each other
- Side step

- Walk backwards
- Use a skipping rope
- Bounce on a trampoline
- Bounce on a spacehopper or a pogo stick
- Swing high on the swings
- Paint the sky with your arms
- Wobble from side to side
- Wobble forwards and backwards
- Choose a song and dance to it
- Throw and catch a ball or bean bag to someone else
- Roll a ball to each other
- Give out books in class
- Carry a bag of books from one place to another

13. Activities

Five super powers

Ask the child to trace around their hand on paper or card (or they could, for example, make a paint handprint) and write their name across the palm. Encourage the child to write a 'super power' they have on each finger.

This exercise can help to boost a child's confidence, helping them to identify positives about their individual personality. Children may struggle with this activity at first and may need some help. Talking about things that they admire in others first may help them to begin to talk about positive traits. Talking about super heroes or people that they admire can also be a good way to help with this activity. A child's initial reaction might be that they like a super hero because they shoot people, or can fly – however, when you talk more, you may find that the child also admires how brave the super hero is, or that they like how they take chances, or help others.

Dreamcatchers

Dreamcatchers are traditional symbols that are hung where a person sleeps. Native Americans believed that good and bad dreams float through the air in the night, and that when people sleep under a dreamcatcher the bad dreams are caught in it, before vanishing in the morning sunlight. They believed that the good dreams were caught in the dreamcatchers too, but, because they were good, they could slide down the feathers and float down the dreamcatcher, catching more good energies on their way to the person underneath.

You could ask the child to draw their own dreamcatcher or use the preprinted image here. How you do this might depend on the child's age, ability and time constraints. The child could then simply draw a design on their dreamcatcher, or they could stick feathers and other art materials onto the paper.

Alternatively you could make a dreamcatcher with the child, using, for example, paper plates with wool woven through the middle, decorated with materials such as feathers, tissue paper, pens, pencils, buttons, or other bits and pieces you might have available.

The child could write negative emotions, triggers or experiences, onto the dreamcatcher to 'trap them', and positive memories, dreams, wishes or anything else good on the 'dangly' bits.

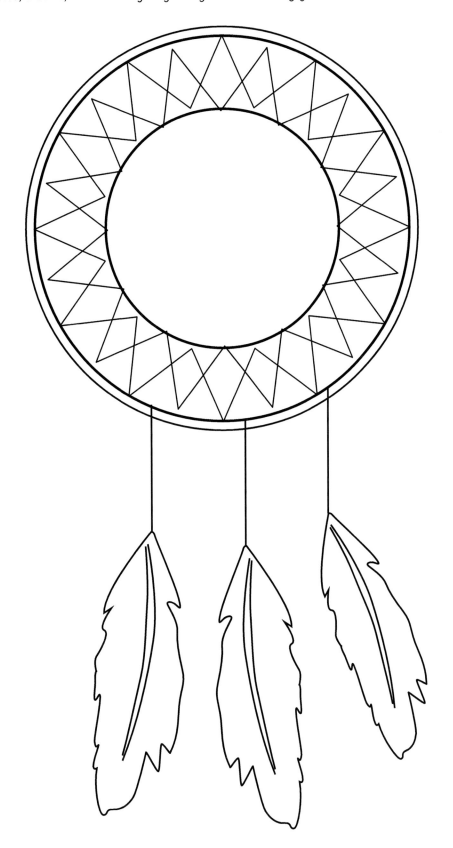

Gratitude

Ask the child to draw around their hand on a piece of paper or card, and on each finger write or draw a picture of something they feel grateful for. As you do this you could use the following script to help explore this with the child.

What are you grateful for? It could be people, places, memories, belongings, experiences, being able to run fast, pets, anything at all that you feel glad about.

When we feel grateful and think positively it can help our brain to change the way it thinks. If we keep helping it to focus on positive things, things we like, that make us feel good, and things we are thankful for, it can begin to learn to do this without any help. When we think positively it can help us to feel more positive and feeling good ... well, feels good.

Practise having a gratitude attitude, the more you practise the easier it will become. We can't feel angry and grateful at the same time – and, I know what I would prefer ...

Support

You will need: a pack of Post-it notes, some coloured pens and a sheet of A3 paper.

Talk to the child about how people can be supported and cared for by all sorts of people. Explain that it is important to have people we can rely on and trust, people who are 'there for us'. Some people have family or friends (or pets) who are there for them. Some people can rely on other people such as teachers, lunchtime supervisors, foster carers, next-door neighbours or social workers. Ask the child to think about who they want to include.

First of all, ask the child to draw themselves on a Post-it note, and to stick the drawing onto the paper wherever they like. Then, using a different Post-it note for each person (or animal) that they feel are 'there for them', they can stick the drawings onto the same piece of paper. Suggest they put each drawing close to the drawing of them if they feel close to the person or animal, and put the drawings further away if they feel not so close. The child can move the Post-it notes around as much as they need to, and they can talk about what they're doing if they feel OK about it.

Inside my head

Ask the child to draw, write, use colour, or cut out words or pictures from magazines to create a collage to help them share what they may be thinking or feeling on the inside. This might include things that they already share with others, such as they love PE and hate maths, and possibly the things that they keep to themselves and don't tell or show others.

This exercise can be supported by talking to children about how it can help to share their thoughts, feelings and emotions with a person they trust.

Again, as with all exercises, it may be that this is not the right time, or you may not be the right person, or children may feel too vulnerable to do this. Children might not express much during this exercise, however just having this discussion can help them to understand the importance of sharing their feelings, and they may then remember this at a later date when they are feeling more able to share. It can also help children to reflect on what they don't share with others too, which can promote change later.

Children could use the outlines on the following pages to create their collage.

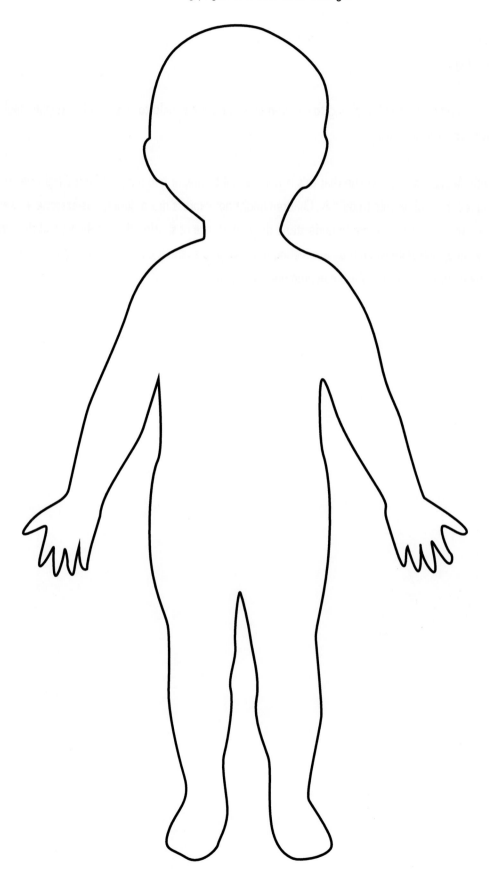

Snakes and ladders

Playing games with children can be a powerful and fun way of building a relationship, as well as rapport and trust. It can help with learning about turn-taking and winning and losing.

Adding some additional tasks into an already established game can be a good way of helping children to express themselves in a less intrusive and less intense manner. For example, when playing snakes and ladders you could agree before starting that: when you land on a snake, before you go down it, you have to give an example of something that makes you feel sad or angry and when you land on a ladder, before you can move up it, you have to give an example of what you could do if you were feeling sad or angry. These are just some examples, but you can use whatever you feel may be helpful to explore with the child.

Telling their story

Helping children to tell their own stories can be very powerful for them, and can help them to make sense of their life or certain events. If you are already aware of what has happened to them, it can also be helpful for you to understand what the child *believes* happened. There can often be a disconnection between reality and what the child remembers or has created in place of actual knowledge. This can be an opportunity to gently explain events and explore them with the child, which might help them make some sense of them and gain a better understanding.

This needs to be done *very* gently and carefully, as, after all, this is *their* reality or memory. It also needs to be done slowly. So you will need to make sure that there is enough time available to do this (even if you plan to do it in stages) *and* that the child is sufficiently supported afterwards, as it can bring up many emotions.

For some children this may be too much and a less intrusive option is to encourage the child to share their story with you, to express it, to see it visually, and to be able to talk about it without exploring it more factually. It may be that there is no one who is really aware of the actual events in a child's life, and/or that their memories do not need to be explored in order for them to be more factually accurate, as you don't feel that this would be helpful for the child.

Below are some examples of how both of these activities can be carried out with children. However, the child may wish to come up with their own approach to how to represent this – and again working with the child's own ideas and metaphors can be even more powerful.

Life story

You could help the child to create a life storybook, or create one on their behalf. This can be particularly helpful for children who have experienced changes within their lives, such as moving house or schools, living with different people, or various other changes or events. Creating a book can help children to piece together the events in their lives, and create an opportunity to reflect on. and gain understanding of, what they have experienced. There are many things that could be included: for example, photographs, letters, drawings, maps of areas, local information leaflets, and anything else you can think might help to illustrate a child's life.

Life story map

Creating this on a large piece of paper, or a roll of paper can mean that children can actually 'walk their path', stopping at various parts to explore them or share.

They can move backwards and forwards through time, and quickly move past parts they aren't yet ready to explore – giving them a full view of their life and the autonomy to explore it however they wish.

This can be created using drawings, words, symbols, colours – whatever makes sense to the child.

Tree of life

It can be helpful when carrying out this activity to take a child outdoors into nature to see a tree stump, where you can talk about how its rings develop over time. Or take a piece of wood outside with you where there are other trees – this gives the child the opportunity to hear the explanation about a tree's life and tree rings with the visuals all around them. Being outside, with nature, can also be relaxing and allow the child to feel freer to express themselves; and, again, kinaesthetic learning can help them in many ways. (Kinaesthetic learning is when learning is through practical, hands on, physical activities.)

Use the outline below to ask children to show what story their tree rings might tell about them. This can be done using words, sentences, colours, shapes – or whatever else the child might wish to use.

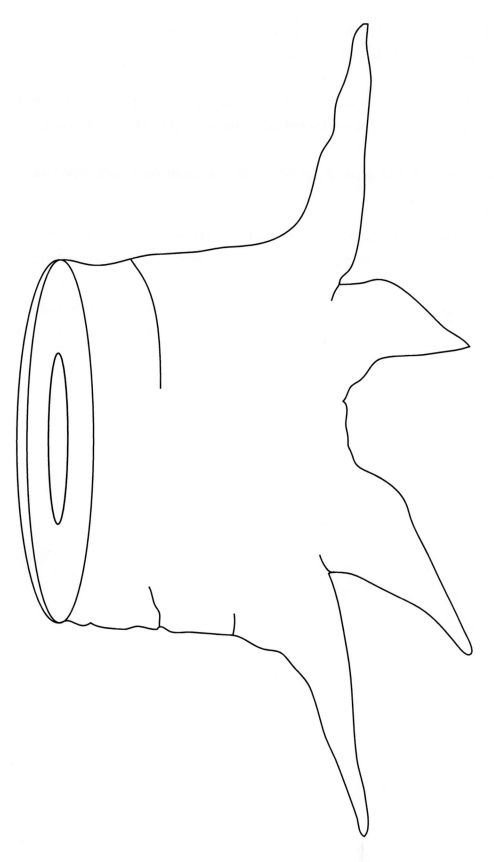

What do you carry?

In the accompanying storybook, Ava carries a trunk with her. Have a discussion with the child about what they think might be in Ava's trunk. Talk to them about how we all carry our feelings and memories with us wherever we go. If we carry good feelings we can feel light and happy inside, but if we carry things that make us sad or angry we can sometimes feel heavy, as if we're carrying a heavy bag with us. Ask the child: 'If you put your feelings in a trunk like Ava's, what do you think would be in there?' Or 'What would you carry in your trunk?' Then the child can draw, colour or write things on Ava's trunk below.

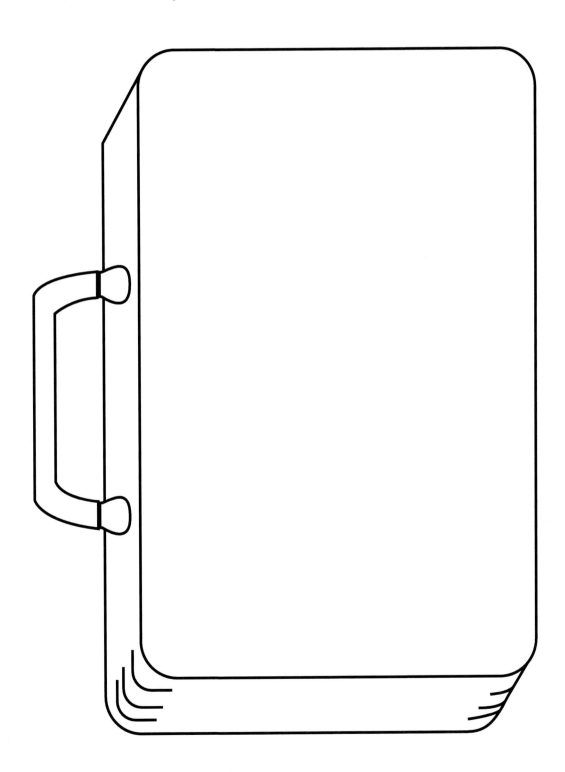

Emotion words

Happy	Cheerful	Satisfied
Lonely	Alone	Terrific
Calm	Delighted	Relaxed
Confused	Silly	Unloved
Afraid	Thankful	Mean
Responsible	Sad	Gloomy
Worried	Grateful	Blue
Uncomfortable	Bored	Frustrated
Destructive	Glad	Disappointed
Furious	Excited	Hurt
Awful	Loved	Embarrassed
Confident	Proud	Scared
Content	Courageous	Miserable
Angry	Ashamed	Kind
Irritated	Quiet	Jealous
Insecure	Curious	Guilty
Shy	Generous	Worried
Surprised	Ignored	Peaceful
Brave	Impatient	Stubborn
Friendly	Interested	Relieved
Overwhelmed	Loving	Energetic

This is an activity designed to help increase the child's emotional vocabulary and to check their understanding of emotion words. It can help us to identify gaps in understanding and know where further work is required to help children make more sense of their emotions.

There are so many different ways to use emotion cards with a child. Below are some suggestions, but please feel free to use them however you and the child wish.

You can make your own cards, or photocopy the words on the previous page onto coloured card for example, cut them out, and even laminate them if you want them to last a long time. This is not an exhaustive list – there are many, many more that can be added, and the children may have suggestions too.

- Choose a card and talk about a time when you have felt like this.
- Choose a card, see if you can make or draw the facial expressions of a person who is feeling like this.
- Group together emotions you feel are positive and emotions you feel are negative.
- Group together angry words, happy words, sad words.
- Choose a card and say how someone might act if they were feeling like this.

For some children this might need to be broken down with pictures of various facial expressions. This can help children to begin to recognise and read facial expressions. However, children who have experienced an insecure attachment may struggle with this. Instead, the child could then start to pair the word cards with the face pictures, for example.

Ask the child what they see in each picture, and help them to break down the expressions. For example, if it was a shocked face, you might note that the person's mouth is wide open, and their eyes may be too, or they may have a hand over their mouth.

Talking about anger

Talking to children about anger is very important. It is essential for them to know that every single person in the whole world has felt angry at some time. A lot of children are taught that anger is bad, and should be hidden rather than expressed, or they may have witnessed people unable to control their anger. When children do act out and express their own anger it can lead to them feeling ashamed, and often scared of an out-of-control expression of emotion. Sometimes children do not express their anger, but turn it inwards towards themselves: such children are often overlooked, and although they're just as angry and hurt as the ones throwing things, we simply don't see them.

It can be useful to talk to children about anger being a cover-up feeling for other emotions – feelings such as fear, sadness, loneliness, shame, disappointment, frustration and guilt can be hiding behind anger. Offer an example of this to the child: for example, this could be when you lost at a game and became angry, but now you can see that it was really disappointment that was hiding behind anger. Ask them if they can think of a time when one of their other emotions hid behind anger.

It is important for children to understand that anger is as important an emotion as being happy or sad or excited, and that there are ways we can express anger without hurting ourselves or others, and without breaking things.

It is also useful to talk about how we might carry anger around with us when we don't deal with it properly – using the metaphor of carrying a big bag of rocks with us can be helpful. Each heavy rock could represent one of the things that make us angry. Talk about how carrying that heavy bag with us everywhere we go can be really hard and tiring, and can make us even more angry and irritable.

This could even be recreated with a strong bag, some rocks and stones. The child could identify the things that make them angry, and, if they don't feel that they handle them well, they could be added to the bag. At the end of the activity the child may still be able to carry the bag (particularly when children like to prove how strong they are) – so you could talk about what a pain it would be to have to carry it with them and how it would get in the way when they were on the trampoline, it would take up room in their bed, and it would make them slower when they are running for the football.

Using metaphors with children can be helpful, though try to keep the metaphors simple, so as not to confuse the child. Children may well come up with their own metaphors for their anger, metaphors that, for a child, can be very powerful. Using the children's own metaphors with them can show that you really understand some of how they feel when they are angry. Some children explain that it is like having an eruption – like a volcano, a rocket, or like when you shake up a bottle of fizzy pop. One child I worked with said that it felt like having a monster in her tummy that sometimes took over her thoughts and feelings, and made her say and do horrible things to other people.

You could take the child outside with a plastic bottle of cola and a well-known brand of mints (Google it!) to demonstrate what can happen when things get too much for us to cope with. The mints can represent the things that make them angry, and they could name them before you pour them quickly into the cola (which can represent the child), and watch it fizz up and explode (like when they get angry, shout, hurt someone or break things). Make sure the child is not near to the bottle!

Using activities that are 'hands on' for children can really help with their learning. It help them to remember what they have learned, and can also give you something to refer back to at a later date, and, of course, they are fun – *bonus!*

Explaining to children that they have the power inside them to control their anger can come as a surprise to some; it can also be empowering, and for some it can become a challenge.

Using a second packet of mints you could talk through the child's anger triggers one at a time, asking them what they could do instead of keeping them inside and letting them explode like the bottle of cola. If the child isn't able to name alternatives you could ask them to think about what they might say to a friend or classmate. Sometimes children find it easier to think about alternative actions when they can remove themselves from the situation, or think about it from the point of view of helping another person. This can make it easier for the child to think objectively, something that is often not possible when thinking about their own anger.

You could also try this next activity if the child isn't scared of balloons popping (but check this out first). You might both want to wear safety goggles too. Using a balloon and a pump to demonstrate anger, ask the child to tell you something that makes them feel angry. Each time they tell you a reason, pump some air into the balloon – keep going until the balloon explodes, like our anger does when we end up shouting, or lashing out, or 'exploding'. Some children really enjoy this activity, and, because of the excitement of the balloon getting bigger and bigger and eventually popping, it is an activity I find resonates with the child – and they can remember it when they begin to feel angry, prompting them to find a more positive way to let it out.

'Now I know that I can do something else with my angry feelings. It doesn't always work, but sometimes it does.' – 7-year-old boy

Matching

Pre-planning with children can help them to understand that there are things they can do to help them to take care of themselves when they experience different emotions. This forward thinking can help children to feel that they have a plan. It can empower them to make changes, and can help them to choose one of the options to deal with an emotion when they might otherwise feel overwhelmed by it.

When I feel _____ I can _____ to help to take care of myself.

Examples might include:

- When I feel SAD I can IMAGINE I AM HUGGING SOMEONE I CARE ABOUT to help take care of myself.
- When I feel HAPPY I can LAUGH AND HAVE FUN WITH MY FRIENDS to help take care of myself.
- When I feel ANGRY I can TAKE DEEP BREATHS to help take care of myself.

How do you feel?

You can help children to share their emotions, or to 'check in' with themselves in various ways. There are some suggestions below. You may find that the child prefers one over another, and it may be trial and error until they connect with something. These activities may feel odd to the child at first, as they are not used to noticing their internal feedback, or to having someone ask for this information. But if you persevere, you might just find an emotional 'language' that the child can understand.

If it is appropriate, you could ask the child how they are feeling before and then again after taking part in an activity. This can help them to become more aware of how expressing themselves can change their emotional state, and therefore 'prove' that it works – which, in turn, can encourage children to continue to do something.

There are many other ways of doing this. Feel free to get creative with it, and include the child in coming up with new ways of expressing and noticing changes in their moods, emotions and feelings.

Children might find a visual indication like the one on the previous page easier to use – they could even make their own.

Colours and shapes can be ways for a child to describe their feelings, and the adults don't necessarily need to know what colours or shapes mean (unless the child wishes to explain their thought processes). The important thing is that the child is aware of the *change* in colour or shape and what it means for them.

- 'What colour is your mood?'
- 'What shape is your mood?'
- 'What is the weather like outside?' (Weather can be used to describe feelings, for example thunder storms, sunshine, or anything in between.)
- 'What is the weather like inside your head or body?'
- 'Number how you are feeling right now?' (0 is the worst they could feel and 5 is the best they could feel. Or use 0 to 10 where 10 is the calmest, and 0 is the least calm they could be.)

Communicating emotions

There are many ways that children can let adults know how they are feeling. Often children like to have a visual aid to help them to communicate. Children could create an emotions key ring or simply use a time-out card.

Time-out cards can be useful when children start to notice that they are becoming overwhelmed by emotion. They can simply show it to an adult or put it on the kitchen fridge or teacher's desk, indicating to the adult that the child needs some time out of the situation. This could be somewhere completely outside the situation, or, if this is not possible, in a place where they can feel safe and can calm down. They could also use their calm box.

Adults can also identify when the child might need to use their time-out card. This could be done, for example, by showing the child a time-out card, by pointing to the child's time-out card, or by simply saying to the child something along the lines of 'I think it might be a good time to use your calm box'. You might also want to be more explicit with the reasons for this, for example 'I can see your fists are clenched tightly. I think it might be because Joe took your turn, and you are feeling angry, let's get your calm box.'"

This depends entirely on the child and the situation.

An emotions key ring can be used in a similar way, however it is more specific about the emotion a child is experiencing. The emotions key ring can also help children to extend their emotional vocabulary. You could help the child to make their own key ring by choosing pictures or images together that the child feels represent different emotions. The child could draw their own images if they wished, though do make sure they are pocket-sized. You might also wish to write the emotion onto the image to help people to identify what it means to the child.

Once you have images for a variety of emotions, cut them out separately, laminate them for durability, and use a hole punch so they can be attached to a key ring. The child might wish to keep this in their pocket or in their desk at school. The child can then share their emotions with others by showing them a specific image.

'I use my superman time-out card when I feel changes in my body. My teacher lets me sit in the reading corner for a few minutes until I can join in again.' – Year 2 child

14. Additional support

Counselling

Ensuring that a child has access to the right mental health support means that their needs can be assessed, and the child can be supported appropriately by therapists who are specifically trained in the area of developmental trauma. When children have experienced trauma they very often require further intervention such as counselling in order to help them to process their emotions and experiences.

There are certain techniques that counsellors are trained to use with children, particularly where there is complex trauma or Post-traumatic Stress Disorder present, in order to support their mental health.

As we already know, when children have experienced trauma it can be difficult for them to engage in relationships, and, due to their experiences, they may also already be suspicious of strangers, professionals in particular. Supporting the child to feel safe enough to access counselling is a very important part of how you can help in this process.

Continuing to be a consistent and reliable key person for the child will work well alongside any counselling, and will help to support the work that the therapist is doing. The therapist may ask that no direct work with emotions takes place when the child is accessing therapy; however this should be considered on a case-by-case basis, and can be discussed with the therapist before sessions begin. For therapy to be most effective it needs to be included in an approach that home, school and the therapy are all using.

The reality is that counselling will not continue indefinitely, and often there may be extended periods of time when the child is not seeing the therapist, for all sorts of different reasons. The relationship with the counsellor is contained within the therapy session, and the child will continue to require support outside of the sessions, and this is why having a key person is so important for a child.

Self-care

'Never work with children or animals' is a famous saying that I never really understood until I started working with children. It can be one of the most rewarding things you can do, but supporting children and young people can also be hard. Supporting children and young people who have additional needs can be even harder.

Being with children who have emotional outbursts, find relationships difficult, act out (behaving impulsively as a way of venting painful or uncomfortable emotions), or withdraw can feel impossible at times. A child who has experienced trauma can display some of the most challenging and often baffling behaviour, appearing bossy, controlling, manipulative, clingy, withdrawn and destructive. To cope with such behaviour and continue with the relationship, we as adults need to keep in mind that they are also out of the child's control. Such behaviour is not about us, and is not a personal attack. The child is simply trying to get their needs met. We need to consider what the need is and what the child is communicating. Often the people closest to the child experience the most challenging behaviours. There's a bit of a back-handed compliment in there somewhere!

The behaviours children display can bring up many emotions in the adults around them. Remaining connected to the child, as well as calm and responsive, can be difficult, particularly when our own attachment experiences are brought into play – which they inevitably are. Adults can be left feeling many things – resentful, hopeless, hurt, frustrated, let down, helpless – and we are often left doubting ourselves. We need to consider that the emotions we're experiencing may actually be how the child is feeling. Reflect on this: could you be getting a sense of what the child is experiencing? Alternatively these may be very much your own feelings: consider how you can be supported so that you can manage them. Reflecting on our own feelings and triggers can help us to understand why we respond in certain ways. This can in turn help us to identify areas where extra support is needed, and so to respond differently in the future with a new sense of awareness.

Despite all of this, we stay. We keep going back for the children. The very same children who can leave us feeling emotionally exhausted are the very reason we don't just give up. Because they are vulnerable and need someone rooting for them, someone who cares, and, most importantly, someone who doesn't just give up like others may have done before. That is why we stay.

Working with children can be emotionally, spiritually and physically draining and I can't stress how important it is to look after ourselves. On a plane, you have to put on your own oxygen mask first before helping others to put theirs on, and this is a really useful metaphor to remember. We can't help, support or care for others, unless we are doing all of the above for ourselves.

In the past I have been guilty of neglecting myself, and, for example, when it came to my annual leave I would regularly end up with tonsillitis or the flu. This was my body telling me, 'You won't rest? I'll *make* you rest!' Almost as if it was a challenge, my body would conjure up a horrible illness to make me stay in bed.

Although I knew this, and each time would resolve to make changes, I continued the same cycle year on year until I knew it couldn't continue. I couldn't continue.

Self-care can feel alien to those of us in a caring, supporting role (how ironic). It is often the case that those drawn to working with vulnerable people are notoriously poor at caring for themselves. So often we are the rescuers, who want to fix everything and feel a sense of reward from helping others, even if it is at our own expense. We spend our days encouraging children to ask for help, showing them they can rely on others for support, and telling them that expressing how they feel is perfectly acceptable, yet we don't follow our own advice. I bet that this is the least read section in this book, and people will be tempted to skim over it ... if they even read it at all – yes, you know who you are!

Self-care is different for everyone: for some people it is going for a quick jog, for others a weekly counselling session, hours at the gym, a walk, or a phone call with their best friend. It doesn't matter what it is, it just matters that you find what works for you, and you do it – regularly.

There are strategies and tools in this book that can also be used to help you to look after yourself. Practise them with the child you are supporting, and then use them yourself. Model self-care to the young minds that you support. How can we expect children to believe in these tools, if we don't believe in them ourselves? Add some 'items' to your own 'back pack' – and use them.

It sounds corny, I know, but a little bit of care goes a long way, and a lot can last an entire childhood. Be there, for them. Be there, for you. *It's worth it, honest!*

Further information

There are many books and websites where you can find further information about supporting children who struggle with the impact of insecure attachment or trauma. I have suggested a few that may be beneficial.

Heather Geddes (2006). *Attachment in the Classroom: A Practical Guide for Schools.* London: Worth Publishing.

Louise Bomber (2007). *Inside I'm Hurting: Practical Strategies for Supporting Children with Attachment Difficulties in Schools.* London: Worth Publishing.

John Bowlby (2005). *A Secure Base.* London: Routledge.

www.attach.org ATTACh website has information about the importance of attachment.

www.innerworldwork.co.uk is a website promoting a 'Trauma Informed Schools Campaign' with helpful videos.